No More Robots

Constance Russell and Justin Dillon
General Editors

Vol. 2

The [Re]Thinking Environmental Education series
is part of the Peter Lang Education list.
Every volume is peer reviewed and meets
the highest quality standards for content and production.

PETER LANG
New York • Bern • Frankfurt • Berlin
Brussels • Vienna • Oxford • Warsaw

Bob Coulter

No More Robots

Building Kids' Character, Competence, and Sense of Place

PETER LANG
New York • Bern • Frankfurt • Berlin
Brussels • Vienna • Oxford • Warsaw

Library of Congress Cataloging-in-Publication Data

Coulter, Bob.
No more robots: building kids' character, competence,
and sense of place / Bob Coulter.
pages cm. — ([Re]thinking environmental education; vol. 2)
Includes bibliographical references.
1. Place-based education. 2. Environmental education.
3. Moral education. I. Title.
LC239.C68   370.11'5–dc23   2014002009
ISBN 978-1-4331-2472-3 (hardcover)
ISBN 978-1-4331-2471-6 (paperback)
ISBN 978-1-4539-1305-5 (e-book)
ISSN 1949-0747

Bibliographic information published by **Die Deutsche Nationalbibliothek.**
Die Deutsche Nationalbibliothek lists this publication in the "Deutsche
Nationalbibliografie"; detailed bibliographic data are available
on the Internet at http://dnb.d-nb.de/.

© 2014 Peter Lang Publishing, Inc., New York
29 Broadway, 18th floor, New York, NY 10006
www.peterlang.com

Table of Contents

Acknowledgments

This work builds on much of my career, first as an elementary grade teacher, and later as one who works to support teachers and kids as they build their own experiences. To that end, I owe a great deal to the late Kirsten Kaiser, a legendary teacher at the Common School in Amherst, MA, and to David Sobel, an equally prominent member of the faculty at Antioch University New England. Where I am as a teacher grows out of the seeds they helped to nurture. Also, many thanks are due to Alan Feldman, who helped me launch the second phase of my career, helping teachers to find the space where they can continue to grow past our time together. Throughout my career I've been privileged to work with many inspirational colleagues. Learning together with them has helped to shape the messages in this book.

On a more practical note, I would like to acknowledge the National Science Foundation and the Litzsinger Road Ecology Foundation. What is contained here may or may not reflect their official positions, but their support has enabled this work to unfold and mature over time. For that, I owe a debt of gratitude. Also, thanks to the Missouri Botanical Garden for providing the professional autonomy to explore these ideas.

Finally, and most importantly, I'd like to dedicate this work to the thousands of kids I've been entrusted with over the years. Many thanks for the insights and fun you offer, and for sharing your sense of wonder as life unfolds for you.

Restoring the Craft
of Teaching and Learning

T his book emerges from an enigma. For six years I served as the principal investigator and project director for two projects funded by the National Science Foundation (NSF) investigating aspects of STEM (science, technology, engineering, and mathematics) learning. Both projects had a roughly similar focus: In partnership with MIT, we hired teachers and other professionals from schools in the St. Louis and Boston areas to lead after-school and summer programs with kids ages 10 to 13. The two projects—Local Investigations of Natural Science (LIONS) and Community Science Investigators (CSI)—each had a focus on local, community-based investigations. We provided intensive professional development and ongoing support for the teachers that included help in locating resources, consultation on their project designs, and co-teaching as requested by the teachers. Rather than imposing one program on everyone, areas of focus were at the discretion of each teaching team. This choice was driven both by a desire to help teachers become the designers of students' experiences and by a practical consideration of the school location. If the kids were to be involved in their local community, projects had to reflect what was available in the neighborhood. Project examples included monitoring water quality in local streams, investigating demographic change in a community over three generations, and assessing how easy it is for community members to have access to healthy food. In some cases, projects emerged spontaneously from local high-interest events, such as a study of tornado patterns undertaken by two schools in response to recent tornado strikes in their communities. The important point here is that there was no set curriculum for teachers to follow, which proved to be both a strength and a challenge in the program. Thus, an enigma was born.

In the NSF proposals, we articulated our optimistic belief that the open-ended scope of the projects would enable teachers to teach from their passions, which would in turn ignite strong youth interest in STEM investigations. In all too many schools in the United States, teachers are held to a script, with their pedagogic decisions determined by a pacing chart for which they have had little—if any—involvement in its development. With their curriculum scripted in this manner, teachers don't have the flexibility to bring in their own personal interests, or to modify the curriculum in response to students' interests. Instead, teachers are expected to "stay on script" and cover the prescribed topics in a specific number of days, regardless of students' learning. The process is a sprint for coverage, memorably captured by the lament I heard from one teacher that she had a week to cover the oceans in her science class. The ideal teacher is increasingly what sociologist C. Wright Mills (1959/2000) described as a "cheerful and willing robot," (p. 171) complying with the norms provided by state and district administrators. In turn, students are expected to engage in similarly robotic compliance, faithfully following their teachers' lead toward a very narrow definition of success—ever higher test scores.

To counter this mechanistic approach to teaching, we built LIONS and CSI on the premise of giving teachers the freedom to bring their own interests into the curriculum and to build projects that are responsive to students' interests. We assumed that providing a project space that was free from accountability and testing constraints would open the doors to rich, personally meaningful STEM investigations. In practice, this happened in some instances but not others. Some teachers created dynamic investigations such as a study of local bird species and which habitats they were most commonly found in, while others remained in the traditional teacher-centered, lesson-based approach to teaching. This latter group of teachers was generally respected by their peers as capable practitioners within the traditional norms of school, but they were persistently unable to conceptualize and structure community-engaged learning opportunities. Instead, they relied on project staff to provide packaged activities to fill each meeting of their group, demonstrating something of a "deer in the headlights, don't know which way to go" approach to planning once they were freed from pre-scripted curriculum. These were teachers from the same district, and in some cases from the same school as teachers who were better able to work "off script" in creating learning opportunities within the community. Demographically the teachers were similar in age and teaching experience, and they were provided with the same levels and types of professional development and follow-up support. Still, there was a persistent gap in how they approached their work.

Since I had many opportunities to be out in the schools with the teachers, I intuitively captured this split as I went from school to school. My hunch was subsequently confirmed in the data that were being collected by our external evaluators. Focus groups, surveys, and interviews all pointed toward differences in practice for the teachers that, in turn, had impacts on levels of student engagement and enthusiasm. The evaluators and I started developing tentative hypotheses about what might be driving this difference in how teachers worked, with a goal of seeing if it was an idiosyncratic quirk in that pool of teachers or if there are in fact significant differences in how teachers approach their work. Fast-forward a year: I received a call from a subcontractor the evaluation team used to collect data for the second year of the project. The gist of the call was, "Hey Bob, we have this odd pattern in the data . . . . Am I missing something?" Again, we saw the difference in how teachers approach their work appearing with a new group of teachers, identified by an evaluator who was not privy to our preliminary framing of the gap.

At this point we gained confidence that we were on to something worthy of further exploration. Despite demographically similar teacher characteristics and similar student populations, some teachers were able to create dynamic, locally engaged learning environments that held students' interest and built a sustaining energy while others created a more passive environment based on a programmed "teach by numbers" approach. More specifically, the dynamic teachers integrated resources from the professional development workshops with their own materials and what they could find in the community, while the others brought virtually nothing of their own interests or community resources, and struggled to implement even comparatively scripted environmental education projects such as tracking signs of seasonal change with Journey North or collecting data on schoolyard bird populations using the FeederWatch projects from the Cornell Lab of Ornithology.

To be clear, this comparison is not meant to demean largely pre-structured environmental projects like these. In fact, Journey North and FeederWatch were offered to the teachers as resources precisely because they were reliable staples of my own teaching when I was an elementary grade science teacher. They have the potential to support great learning experiences in themselves, and can serve as transition tools helping to move teachers and students toward more complex, student-designed environmental projects. The concern here is that even with the extensive scaffolding these projects offer, many teachers still found it difficult to break out of the traditional sequential lesson, classroom-focused norms of what it means to be a teacher. Rather, each week's after-school session was a pro forma exercise following the path provided with minimal enthusiasm. As a result, weekly Journey North "Mystery Class" updates were read for about three-quarters of the spring, before the energy ran out. No effort was made to build toward a culmination, which is where the real power of the project is found, as students use the clues provided from distant cities in comparison with local data to discern the mystery locations. Instead, it was just a lesson in collecting and recording data, but with no substantive purpose. Similarly, bird feeders were hung (and replenished when I brought new seed), but no citizen science data were collected or reported, let alone downloaded from the larger Cornell Lab of Ornithology databases. The experimental protocols that the Cornell project uses to ensure comparable data were absent, depriving the kids of the opportunity to gain an understanding of how science works. As with the Mystery Class implementations, these less successful after-school programs had loosely coordinated activities but little in the way of a strategic alignment toward a purpose.

Experience on these two projects and others that were similar in their operations confirmed my experience from an analysis that colleagues at TERC and I conducted in the early days of the Internet (Feldman, Konold, & Coulter, 2000). In that work, we found that despite all of the enthusiastic hype at the time over the educational promise of "going online," projects can be quite passive experiences if they are pursued without enthusiasm and interest on the part of the teacher. Teachers need to model active curiosity that invites student engagement and ownership of the project, and not just teach a lesson. More than ten years later, despite the rapid growth of cyberculture, the patterns remain the same. As co-author of that study Cliff Konold noted, if there is no appetite for using data as a sense-making tool, all of the professional development, curriculum design efforts, and technological developments engineered to support inquiry won't help.

As a more specific example showing the difference in how teachers approached their own learning, picture a pair of workshops we held in the summer between the two years we were working with a particular cadre of teachers in the LIONS program. The professional development design for that project consisted of an introductory week-long workshop, follow-up support through monthly meetings and one-on-one consultation in the coming year, and a synthesizing "next-steps" workshop the following summer. For the culminating workshop in the second summer, the teachers' vacation and summer school schedules didn't allow everyone to participate at the same time, so we ran two iterations of the same workshop, each intended to help teachers integrate what they learned in the first year and plan for the coming year. It so happened that teachers who were generally more passive were able to attend one week, while most of those who showed more curricular ambition were able to attend the other week. (There are of course benefits to integrating the groups, but in this case the teachers' schedule constraints that summer precluded such an arrangement. All of the other professional development experiences included the full group of teachers.)

One of the tools we introduced for both groups was a new version of MITAR, an augmented reality software tool developed by our project partners at MIT. Augmented reality (AR) software allows students to investigate local community issues with the help of handheld computers or smartphones. Imagine exploring a local environmental issue, guided by the GPS capability of your smartphone. As you approach each key location, you are guided to observe the real world, with your experience supplemented by information that pops up on your phone once you are at that location. For the first (more passive) group of teachers, we went out to a local park and tried a sample investigation. Most of the teachers were intrigued with the potential, and asked if I could come and "do this" with their students. (The translation here is "do this in place of me," which would be fine if it were a starting point for teachers to gradually assume ownership.) A few weeks later the second workshop took place. As sometimes happens, we fell behind schedule and didn't get out to try the activity, primarily as a result of the rich professional exchanges the teachers were having, sharing what they had done at their school the previous school year. While the first workshop had teachers working in a "receive" mode, the second one had much more of a co-creative feel to it. In any event, all we had time for that first day was a very brief introduction to the software and distribution of a book on uses of augmented reality in education by Eric Klopfer (2008), who was co-principal investigator on the LIONS and CSI projects and lead developer of the MITAR software. We ended the day agreeing to jump into AR the next morning. Imagine my surprise to start the next day with all of the teachers having already started flipping through the book and having downloaded the software on their own. Some had already started "mousing" around with it on their home computer as well.

While it would be easy to say that some found the augmented reality tools appealing and others didn't, this was just indicative of the persistent split in the teacher population we worked with. Some jumped in and forged opportunities, while others waited for the next direction. Viewed more broadly than these projects, this gap seems endemic to the profession. Based on collegial interactions in the first half of my career (when I worked as an upper elementary grade teacher) and in my subsequent work leading teacher professional development initiatives for the Missouri Botanical Garden, this difference is all too present. Teachers who are more successful in leading active, project-based, community-engaged studies exhibit a degree of reflexivity (defined by Wikipedia as "an act [that] 'bends back on,' refers to, and affects the entity instigating the action") that simply isn't nearly as common among teachers less interested or less able to create these dynamic learning environments. In short, the reflexive teachers built capacity over time, using each experience and resource to raise their capacity for future endeavors. We saw this in how the teachers drew on what they had done prior to starting our partnership, and in how what they did early in our work together resurfaced in new and more complex designs later on. Over the course of our time with them, the highly reflexive teachers built after-school and summer programs that increased in energy over time, whereas the less reflexive teachers moved forward from week to week, offering generally credible but all too often rather pro forma projects for their students. Also, the reflexive teachers were more successful in achieving a related goal for LIONS and CSI as they were much more likely to have applied what they learned with us about community-focused, project-based learning back into their "regular" school day teaching assignments. In this way, the net impact of the difference in teaching approaches went beyond the after-school setting to affect all of the students the teachers worked with.

Thus, I was compelled to write this book: an effort to synthesize what we have learned through LIONS, CSI, and other initiatives supporting place-based education about how teachers who are more successful in creating STEM-rich local investigations go about their work, and how their approach differs from that taken by teachers less able to create such environments. If the book were a novel, the protagonist would be the adventurous teacher working zealously to overcome the obstacles to place-based education (and there are many, as we will see!). The villain isn't the other teachers, administrators, or parents as individuals. For the most part they are dedicated and want to do their jobs well. Rather, the villain here is the collection of norms about school and about childhood, and the policies that emerge from these norms. Left unchallenged, these norms reward and at times enforce a passive, disengaged learning environment for both teachers and students that too often lead to the robotic approach Mills (1959/2000) criticized. To build spaces where place-based education and similar initiatives can thrive, we need to think differently about how we pursue education. Simply moving to a new reform is not going to work any more than the litany of reforms that have come before. The best plot analogy I can make appears in the book *Flatland* by Edwin Abbott (1994). In that work, everyone is living in a flat, two-dimensional environment until some brave souls get adventurous and realize that there is a third dimension. Still, many characters in Abbott's novel want to stay down in their comfort zone. Similarly, we have a gap in the teaching profession between those who go with the norms of passivity and those who build toward more active, student-driven learning projects of which place-based education is an example. Despite the odds, some teachers break through to a new dimension of practice.

In the pages ahead, we will explore the dynamics at work when teachers take this more active stance toward their pedagogy and practice, and identify the far more common forces that serve to maintain traditional classroom norms. After an introductory chapter on place-based education and its progressive roots, we'll look at how active place-based education enables significantly different experiences for students. Building on this base, the second half of the book explores how the teachers who lead these experiences see their work and the kids they serve differently. Taken as a whole, the book is an exercise in the use of what C. Wright Mills (1959/2000) called the "sociological imagination," an effort to describe how individual actors, their surrounding cultural histories, and prevalent social structures interact to give shape and meaning to what people do. Methodologically, it reflects an abductive process, which Timmermans and Tavory (2012, p. 167) describe as using a "dialectic between data and generalization as a way to account for empirical findings." Relatedly, others describe abduction as a process leading toward "inference to the best explanation" (Lipton, 1991). In simpler terms, the book is an effort to describe and place in a useful analytic context a set of empirical observations of kids and teachers at work. The book ends with an effort to use our sociological imagination to envision an alternative to our current path, one that gives teachers and students the space and capacity to be effective learners, with adults and youth jointly building character, competence, and a sense of place. The challenges we face locally and globally require no less a vision for education. It is time for schools to move out of Flatland and see new possibilities.

Overview of the Book

If you're like me, you may be standing at a conference exhibit hall table leafing through this book, or reading an e-book sample online to decide if this book is useful for you. To help answer your questions, I provide a short overview of each chapter's main arguments.

The book opens with a chapter focusing on place-based education as an educational strategy. While in some ways it is new and somewhat trendy in educational circles, place-based education has deep antecedents in educational history. Examples from long-standing progressive schools show how classes of different ages have engaged their local community, illustrating the rich legacy on which modern concepts of place-based education are built. In an effort to provide more than a simple recitation of examples of place-based practice, the first chapter examines these cases analytically, sketching the close alignment place-based education has with progressive educational values. In its emphasis on direct experience, on the collaborative work between the teacher and her students, and in the integration of disciplines, modern place-based projects carry the torch of progressive education in an educational climate that is all too often hostile to these underlying values. In place of active engagement and shared decision making, there is increasing emphasis in too many schools on standardization and algorithmic approaches to teaching and learning. The net result of this trend toward scripted instruction is a pervasive de-skilling of the teaching profession and apathy among students, many of whom have more intellectually stimulating lives outside of school than they do in school. As 11-year-old Ross noted in regard to his augmented reality project, "Making handheld games is a lot different than school because it requires smarter thinking and trial and error × 17. In school you don't get a second trial because when it's done it's done and that's your grade."

To push back against this de-skilling that seems endemic to modern schooling, the opening chapter lays the groundwork for considering place-based education as a definite opportunity to craft a richer learning environment for teachers and students. In one of many applications of John Dewey's educational philosophy we'll be making, we'll draw from his idea of learning as an aesthetic process of engagement (Dewey, 1934/2005), and contrast it with what he appropriately called the "anesthetic" function that traditional norms of schooling impose. More than just a curriculum reform to adopt, place-based education brings a rich array of historical and modern progressive values to the fore. Chapter 1 provides an essential overview of the terrain.

Chapter 2 extends the analysis, offering a student-focused view of place-based education. As you would expect, differences in how teachers approach their work have an impact on students' interest and enthusiasm. Given this, it shouldn't be any great surprise that when teachers show more commitment to neighborhood involvement and shared ownership of the learning, students become more actively engaged in community-based projects. Because of this difference in experience, these students develop over time a level of "action competence" (Jensen & Schnack, 1997) that enables them to pursue comparatively advanced projects. As described more fully in the chapter, increasing levels of action competence enable students to go beyond simple activities thrown into the curriculum to practice a skill or (even more prosaically) to keep things from getting too boring. Instead, action in this context assumes a trajectory toward meaningful outcomes for definable groups of people. So, the students who were motivated by their understanding of tornados to teach younger students about tornado safety, or the students who worked on riparian corridor improvements in response to their growing understanding of community water quality issues were each developing action competence. Of course, there is considerable overlap between action competence and service-learning, which is explored in some depth in this chapter. What I find more appealing in an action competence frame is the greater emphasis placed on students' ownership of the project and the focus on investigating the underlying causes of what they are seeing. With this deeper understanding, students' efforts will more likely be founded on causal analysis and informed by a process of considering several alternative visions. Supported by their teachers, the students reflexively develop capacity as they pursue their work. Clearly this level of student engagement is a desirable outcome, but in our experience it only happens with teachers who themselves exhibit a strong level of agency.

Viewing the learning process more generally, Chapter 2 continues with a look at what kind of learning is possible in an environment that builds toward action competence. Beyond the "banking" metaphor of education advanced by Freire (1993) in which students store knowledge and skills for future use, students who work in a real-world context get access to what Lawler (Lawler & Rushby, 2013) calls "the global inheritance of ideas." Here students learn to traverse the messy complexity of the real world, seeing how different ideas and disciplines help us to see and understand. To provide a rudder for this traversal of the global inheritance, we take a look at a specifically Deweyan approach to inquiry, which provides a strong framework for an otherwise overused term. These strands are tied together at the end of the chapter with a call to "work on the work" in order to ensure that students' efforts have a suitable degree of complexity and are embedded in real issues, and aren't just created as an academic exercise that will be discarded once graded.

Chapter 3 shifts the focus to teachers as it seeks to articulate a model of teacher agency, or more simply a description of how teachers who are more effective in creating rich, community-based learning environments approach their work. It builds on a sociological model of agency offered by Mustafa Emirbayer and Ann Mische (1998), which posits that people make their choices informed by projections of successful outcomes and by interpretations of previous experiences. The teaching applications of the Emirbayer and Mische model are pretty straightforward yet profound: Teachers make a multitude of decisions great and small, informed by their vision of what successful learning looks like, and by their previous experiences. One key difference we find routinely among teachers who build strong place-based programs is in how they craft a vision of learning that motivates their own effort. In turn, that enthusiasm becomes contagious for the kids. This reflects an assumption we used in framing the National Science Foundation proposals, expecting that teachers freed from their school accountability mandates would teach from what they were passionate about. In practice this happened in some cases, for example, the study of bird habitats mentioned earlier, led by an enthusiastic bird-watcher. In contrast, the less successful programs were characterized by a lack of passion, in which teachers weren't able to bring something they cared about deeply to the kids.

A second key variable we found among teachers relating to the Emirbayer and Mische model is in how well these place-based teachers were able to draw on previous experiences. In terms of reflexivity, we have found over the years that teachers who are more successful in moving away from scripted instruction are better able to draw from past experiences and use this to expand their vision and improve their decision making. In turn, this ability to "go to the well" productively enables teachers to build even more engaging learning environments. For a teacher working from a position of agency and autonomy, each year and each project are informed by what went before in terms of project design and the use of community resources.

Paired with the Emirbayer and Mische agency model is a framework offered by Rosemary Luckin (2010), which describes how the availability of resources affects the learning environment. Clearly, teachers and learners don't function in a vacuum—the availability of people, tools, and curriculum resources all come to bear on creating a successful learning environment. With this said, our experience has been that more effective place-based teachers consistently leverage resources to an extent that less effective teachers don't. In the example cited earlier of how different teachers approached the use of augmented reality (AR) with their students, recall that some teachers became quite active in grabbing the software and starting to explore it, while others looked to me as the outside expert to "do" AR for them. As it turned out, not one of these more passive teachers ever embedded AR into their projects, even with multiple offers to come and work with them. A key dividing point in teachers' agency for place-based education is in how well they embrace this multifaceted "surround" of resources that—when used well—can have a major impact on the kids' experiences. The teachers who create the richest projects step into the complexity and use a social intelligence to navigate these resources in ways that others don't. Since the educational systems within which most teachers work don't reward this initiative, it makes the extra effort that some make all the more laudable.

Chapter 4 considers the key teacher issues in more depth. Given the observed difference in teachers' approaches, how can we explain the variation? It's not simply a matter of training and experience. Remember that the teachers in the LIONS and CSI programs (and others we've worked with) were demographically similar in terms of their own teaching experience, their educational backgrounds, and the students with whom they worked. There is something else at work here that is causing teachers to take different approaches. In this chapter I start with the fairly intuitive point that teachers each see their roles differently, but go beyond this to explore how teachers employ these different role definitions in their pedagogic decision making. A teacher focused on student ownership of projects will make different decisions than will a teacher who sees content coverage to be paramount. To make sense of this difference, the chapter draws on the notion of frames as they are articulated by Erving Goffman (1986) and Donald Schon (1983). Frames provide a set of bounds, which help to define the range of choices and the scope of what constitutes an acceptable choice. In practice, these frames make certain decisions preferable, and perhaps even obvious. Imagine a parent who frames her role as one of protecting her child from any possible harm. Inevitably, this child will have a relatively constrained set of experiences in comparison with one whose parent frames her role as helping the child to make good decisions, accepting that kids will occasionally get hurt. As long as the potential injury is modest, this latter parent is willing to support freer exploration, balancing the risk with the benefits of richer experiences. Again, different frames lead to different decisions, which in turn have an impact on experiences whether it's in a parent-child or a teacher-student relationship.

Given this, it becomes important to support teachers in building frames that support the action-oriented learning environment required for place-based education. The second half of the chapter does just that, starting with a look at the work of Melissa Gresalfi and her colleagues (Gresalfi, Barnes, & Cross, 2012) in delineating how teachers function in learning contexts. Key components in the Gresalfi framework include how teachers see the affordances of their environment, their intentions for using that environment to achieve desired ends, and their capacity to actually realize effective use. Teachers whose frames value place-based education are in a position to get more out of the affordances of their environment, have more active intentions (beyond curriculum coverage), and are likely better equipped and motivated to be able to take action. In other words, they exhibit a higher degree of agency than their peers operating in a more traditional frame of classroom teaching. Paired with this, place-based education also depends on teachers having a more complex view of knowledge. Instead of running students through a course of activities to collect facts and develop practical skills, teachers leading a place-based effort tend to see knowledge as more complex and subjective, and work from this perspective in helping their students develop intellectual capacity through their work. This difference in how teachers see knowledge—their personal epistemology—is an important but often overlooked dimension of students' educational experiences. In practice, all of these design elements play out in a certain set of teaching practices we have found to be more characteristic of place-based educators, including working toward ambitious goals, using experiences to help students assemble evidence and build justifications, building shared ownership with students, and navigating community resources in support of the project effectively. The chapter closes with a look at how experiences are designed to reach these goals, looping back to the student experiences described in Chapter 2.

Chapter 5 extends the analysis and works toward closure by explicitly linking student experiences to their larger social environment, considering how frames of childhood held by parents, teachers, and schools impact learning opportunities. Both teachers and parents have frames that define a scope for what is appropriate behavior for the children in their care. Likewise, schools as institutions reflect certain frames of childhood, giving marked preference to some norms of behavior over others. Based on these frames, parents, teachers, and administrators make decisions that enable or constrain kids' options. Inevitably, this adult framing in turn links to how children see their role: The child of an authoritarian parent will see his primary role as obeying adult authority (or at times finding ways to subvert it), while the child of a progressive parent will likely feel more supported in independent exploration. This latter child will inevitably "mess up" once in a while, but he isn't likely to frame his experiences by a primary concern for obedience and avoiding consequences the way the first child might.

Given this premise, Chapter 5 considers how students' roles are framed by the decisions made for them (implicitly or explicitly) by the adults in their lives. If the learning environment is founded on students taking *action* in the sense of the word used here (working toward meaningful outcomes for definable people, and not just engaging in activities), students will see themselves as being expected to think deeply, creatively, and competently. This creates a vivid contrast with students growing up in an environment that doesn't assume autonomy and action competence as goals for education. For schools to succeed in fledging active learners we need to move past assuming that kids aren't capable of critical thinking and constructive action, and that they need to be sheltered from every possible harm. The inevitable consequence of these constraints is that kids' experiences are very limited in scope and ambition.

We need to do better, and the book closes by suggesting a way forward. Supporting teachers in their efforts to improve their practice requires ongoing support that embeds but goes beyond what are recognized as best practices in teacher professional development. Thus, among other things we need co-teaching and coaching toward practices shown to be effective (Joyce & Showers, 2002), we need consideration of the personal and social dimensions of teaching as well as the professional aspects (Bell & Gilbert, 1996), and we need strategies for helping teachers understand deeply how learning theory underpins curriculum choices (Adey, 2004). These research-proven aspects of professional development are critical, but they must be informed by a vision of agency for teachers and kids, not just a technical rationality. We need a revitalized sense of what it means to teach and to learn if we are to enable rich, community-based learning. As we have seen in the most dynamic classes, both teachers and kids need to understand and contribute to the underlying rationale for what they are doing. We cannot continue to impose procedures on people and expect robotic compliance. We need more decision makers at the level at which it can make the most difference: in the school, and in the classroom. At all levels, we need decisions to be animated by values that favor long-term, organic learning over short-term compliance and comparison of education's winners and losers.

To that end, the book issues a call to enable craftsmanship in both teaching and learning. As Sennett (2008) argues, there is a great deal more to the notion of craftsmanship than the usual connotation of manual labor done well. Rather, a craftsperson works reflexively toward standards of quality. Quite simply, by working at it—ideally in a community of practice that includes what Luckin (2010, p. 28) calls "the zone of available assistance"—you get better. But, as is evident from the arguments made in the preceding chapters, more than technical-procedural knowledge is required to be a craftsperson. Effective place-based teaching and learning rely on an integration of formal and implicit knowing about kids and learning, and about the local community. This implicit dimension of knowing is resistant to—and perhaps is stymied by—overly formal training in procedures and facts. Rather, there needs to be a process of immersion in the physical and psychic space of meaningful projects that leads to change over time (Claxton, 1997). Framed more generally, we need to shift emphasis away from our current obsession with techne (or formal procedures) and increase attention toward phronesis (or practical wisdom). This practical wisdom in turn is the foundation of the agency needed to be an effective teacher or an engaged student.

CHAPTER 1

Place-Based Education—
Building on a Progressive Legacy

Place-based education is an increasingly common term that is being applied to locally focused projects that get students out of the classroom and into the community. David Sobel (2004) describes it as

> the process of using the local community and environment as a starting point to teach concepts in language arts, mathematics, social studies, science, and other subjects across the curriculum. Emphasizing hands-on, real-world learning experiences, this approach to education increases academic achievement, helps students develop stronger ties to their community, enhances students' appreciation for the natural world, and creates a heightened commitment to serving as active, contributing citizens. Community vitality and environmental quality are improved through active engagement of local citizens, community organizations, and environmental resources in the life of the school. (p. 7)

Developed as a framework intended to be responsive both to the sterile world of textbook-driven lessons and the "gloom and doom" catastrophic framing of some strands of environmental education, place-based approaches to education promise a kid-friendly, academically sound alternative. Through placed-based education's interdisciplinary focus on the community where the kids live, students can integrate a range of experiences, concepts, and skills as they investigate real-world issues and work toward solutions. This helps to make environmental education more than just a space to learn about ecology. Instead, by moving from learning to action, place-based education is a strategy that "helps students learn to take care of the world by understanding where they live and taking action in their own back yards and communities" (Place-Based Education Evaluation Collaborative, 2010, p. 2).

Projects that embrace a place-based approach can be found in urban and rural locations and involve both younger and older students. Topics range from local history to environmental issues. While our focus in this book will be on the environmentally focused projects, it's important at the outset to gain a broader perspective on the values underlying place-based education as a whole. Hence the focus of this chapter is to scope out what place-based approaches offer, and where they stand in the legacy of larger educational initiatives. As we will see, there is a considerable overlap with current and historical efforts to promote a progressive approach to education. To start the discussion, here are a few examples of local projects for which we have had varying levels of involvement over the past few years:

Fifth graders at a local Christian day school wanted to improve the habitat they share with their host church. By conducting research on native plants on our grounds at the Litzsinger Road Ecology Center and working with field guides and other resources from the Missouri Department of Conservation, the kids crafted a fairly detailed plan for a small native plant garden adjacent to their playground. Working with Mary Voges, our horticulture supervisor, the fifth graders modified their plans to accommodate fairly nuanced concerns about the level of sunlight available and the suitability of their plant choices for the soil type found in the garden. From there, the students got dirty and planted their garden. Fifth grade students in subsequent years have continued the tradition, identifying new plants where needed to fill out the garden, and looking at possible extensions of the garden to encompass more of the school grounds.

Seventh and eighth graders in a racially mixed, lower-middle-class suburb of St. Louis worked with breaking data not yet released to the general public charting the path of recent tornado strikes. Using geographic information system (GIS) software, they mapped the path of destruction that just the week before had leveled a number of homes and businesses in close proximity to the school. This after-school science club investigation sparked an interest among the students in placing Missouri within the mesh of national tornado data (*Which states have the most? When do they strike most often?*) and led to an effort to raise funds to help those affected by the local storms.

Middle school students in a rural southern Missouri community that is home to a military base conducted research on community resources that would be of interest to families who are stationed at the base. Since many of the students were themselves living in that community because of a parent's deployment at the base, the challenges of relocation and settling into an unfamiliar community were particularly salient and meaningful to the teen researchers. The practice in conducting research in the field and online developed capacities and interests among the students and their teacher that were used in the design of subsequent projects such as an investigation of local water quality concerns that were affecting fishing in the area.

As you can see, projects range in topic and locale, unified by a commitment to meaningful engagement that brings life to learning beyond the textbook.

All of this sounds good, but in an age in which narrow notions of accountability reign, what's the evidence that place-based approaches "work" in support of educational goals? Looking at the cross-program evidence of ten programs representing more than a hundred schools, the Place-Based Education Evaluation Collaborative (PEEC, 2010) found six major benefits associated with engaging kids with their local community as a base for learning. They found that place-based education:

Helps students learn—Starting at a fairly basic level, there is an inherent benefit to be realized when kids get to apply their growing understanding of what they are studying in class. Consistent with other studies that document the academic benefits realized through project-based learning (Polman, 2004), students in a well-designed place-based project have opportunities to learn more deeply and develop a range of skills. A key finding here is that local involvement does not have to come at the cost of academic growth. Instead, it may even promote better thinking than is possible when students are restricted to academic exercises pursued within the classroom environment. As a bonus beyond the academic gains, PEEC evaluation data show increased engagement and enthusiasm for being in school. Given the connection between motivation and learning (Deci & Ryan, 2002) and research showing dissatisfaction and disengagement with traditional schooling (Yazzie-Mintz, 2010), this finding is by itself noteworthy support for place-based education as a catalyst for learning.

Invites students to become active citizens—As noted in the Preface, Jensen and Schnack (1997) described learning environments focused on authentic local issues as real opportunities to develop what they call "action competence," or the skills needed to conceptualize and take on projects that actually make a difference for people. Leveraging this local context is vitally important since it enables first-hand engagement. Instead of simply advocating for a distant cause, authentic local engagement provides the experiential base that Jensen and Schnack deem necessary as a "qualification for being a participant" in the community. If we want to provide intentional, active support for democratic education and see citizenship as more than paying taxes and voting, kids need to be socialized into an environment that nurtures and values civic participation. We will return to this issue in considerable depth in the next chapter, which focuses on students' experiences with place-based education.

Energizes teachers—Chapters 3 and 4 describe in some detail the gap between active, agentic teachers who marshal the resources needed to create dynamic learning environments and their more traditional colleagues. Without the enthusiasm and constructive energy that drive this more ambitious approach to learning, it's easy to fall back on more passive approaches. Dominant paradigms of schooling are all too happy to provide a metaphorical (and at times literal) script to fall back on. For example, I recently completed a professional development workshop with a group of teachers, some of whom were required by their principal to document with an e-mail when they have variations in their lesson plans as minor as a few minutes either way. To avoid the professional entropy endemic to this level of micro-management, the work at hand needs to be valued for its engagement and meaning by the teacher as much as it is by the kids. Rich projects like the ones cited at the beginning of the chapter are much more likely to sustain a teacher's energy level than simply covering each chapter sequentially in a textbook.

Transforms school culture—I recently had the privilege of attending the "launch party" for an outdoor learning center that my staff and I helped to develop at a local school. A key component of that space is a native plant garden built by the third graders, starting with the seeds they collected at our site, "cleaned" (prepared for planting), and then planted at their school site. Making this happen required more than teaching behind closed doors—a model that is all too common in schools. Instead, managing a project at this scale required the teachers to collaborate among themselves as a professional community within the grade and across grade levels, with us as an external partner and with parents who helped with the work and funding. Moving teachers and kids out of isolation and toward joint ventures is a vital educational goal and an important element in building a participatory society.

Connects schools and communities—In another of the after-school projects we supported, a mixed-age group of elementary-grade students reclaimed an old part of the playground to convert to a native plant garden. As part of this effort, they uncovered the remains of a "jungle gym" climbing structure. After the kids presented their project to the district school board, imagine their delight when it drew an anecdote from a board member who had attended that school more than half a century earlier and recalled being caught on top of that structure, too scared to come down. For the kids to imagine a respected 60+-year-old dentist in the community as a scared little boy helped to humanize the whole interaction. (As you might imagine, there was a good bit of banter on this among the school board members, too!) More important, projects like this help to remind the community that education fundamentally is about real live kids, not tables filled with test scores and other performance measures.

Encourages students to become environmental stewards—Whether students are engaged in comparatively simple activities such as a litter pick-up or stream monitoring, or engaging in more consequential actions such as building a bio-retention area to mitigate stream bank erosion, local projects provide the impetus and opportunity for them to become stewards of the environment. While we can wring our hands about deforestation in the Amazon and the "dead zone" in the Gulf of Mexico, projects in which kids can see the difference they are making builds affirmation that they can be stewards of the Earth. As we will see later, a particularly creative high school teacher was actually able to craft a local angle on the "dead zone" for her Midwestern, landlocked students. More generally, through place-based projects fear and anxiety about nature can be replaced with confidence and hope.

In terms of the validity of these PEEC findings, note that there is a substantial overlap here with earlier findings on the benefits of locally integrated environmental education projects. For example, in their seminal report *Closing the Achievement Gap* Lieberman and Hoody (1998) described using the Environment as an Integrating Context (EIC) as an educational framework. As they describe it:

> EIC-based learning is not primarily focused on learning about the environment, nor is it limited to developing environmental awareness. It is about using a school's surroundings and community as a framework within which students can construct their own learning, guided by teachers and administrators using proven educational practices (p. 1).

Similar to the PEEC findings, Lieberman and Hoody cite a range of educational benefits including improved academic, behavioral, and attitudinal results among student participants. In addition, they report positive change for teachers, who found that nearly all of the educators leading the projects were more enthusiastic about teaching, had better interpersonal relationships in the school (with both students and colleagues), developed new content understanding and teaching skills, and tried out new teaching strategies. While there is no implication in the report that the project caused these changes in otherwise disengaged teachers, the positive effect among those who choose to engage in place-based projects is itself noteworthy. In a profession beset with problems of professional burnout and high turnover, approaches that foster continuing revitalization are an important part of the larger effort to strengthen and sustain teachers as professionals.

The important take-away here is that multiple research efforts encompassing diverse settings converge on a similar finding: Connecting kids to their community is a powerful framing for educational experiences. It was this potential that we had in mind back in 2004 when we set out to refocus the efforts of the Litzsinger Road Ecology Center, a field site in suburban St. Louis that is owned by a private foundation and managed by the Missouri Botanical Garden. As the recently appointed director of the center, I had a joint mandate from both the botanical garden and the foundation owning (and largely funding) the site to craft a vision that would revitalize the center's identity and programming. Having completed my master's degree back in the '80s under David Sobel's mentorship at Antioch-New England Graduate School (now Antioch University New England), I sought and followed his advice. From there, my staff and I worked to build a center focused specifically on place-based education. As part of that work we secured the National Science Foundation funding discussed in the Preface, through which the anomaly in teachers' approaches was first noticed and articulated. As you'll recall, we found that some teachers we hired for the after-school and summer programs were able to craft dynamic, engaging learning environments while other teachers with nominally similar backgrounds did not break out of the traditional transmission-focused approach to classroom instruction. In parallel with those NSF-funded after-school efforts, our day-to-day work at the ecology center mentoring other teachers on moving their practice toward community engagement had similar results. Some moved forward into creating revitalized professional identities, while some remained stuck in the more passive status quo.

Taken together, these efforts have provided my staff and me with a decade of iterative experience with the challenges and opportunities of helping individual teachers and whole schools move toward place-based learning. By the end of the book I hope to have shared with you what we have learned about the challenges of change, the characteristics of the teachers who have been able to make that shift, and the impact that place-based learning has on transforming students' learning environment away from the routine of traditional schoolwork. But first we need some context. It's important to remember that place-based education isn't just the latest fad in environmental education. Rather, it builds on and extends a long legacy of progressive approaches to education. To place the work we'll be exploring in the pages ahead within a proper frame of reference, we need to follow Sherlock Holmes's advice to a naive detective and "Read it up—you really should. There is nothing new under the sun. It has all been done before."

The broader scope and history of progressive education as a school reform strategy is beyond the realm of this volume, but it's important to note that a legacy of place engagement runs through that history. As Hutchison (2004) notes, back in the 19th century "(t)hrough lessons in map- and model-making . . . Pestalozzi pioneered the study of place in childhood by having his students explore the terrain and topography of local ecosystems" (p. 84). This emphasis on using models to construct understanding of local ecosystems (rather than relying on generic textbook descriptions of hypothetical spaces) continued in the work of Lucy Sprague Mitchell in her classic work *Young Geographers*, first published in 1934. In a Foreword that was first published in the 1963 edition of the book, Charlotte Winsor (Mitchell, 1963/2001, p. 103) described the work as offering "contents and methods by which teachers can develop children's knowledge of their world based on relationships among facts of their physical environment and between the environment and themselves." Mitchell herself declares that "in curriculum planning the dominating logic should be of the children's experiences and not the subject matter, and that their environment furnishes a field for explorations and discoveries" (Mitchell, 1963/2001, p. 8).

This legacy of geospatial analysis continues today in technologically enriched studies of place relying on use of GIS software (Audet & Ludwig, 2000) and in mobile augmented reality games played on handheld computers and smartphones (Dikkers, Martin, & Coulter, 2012; Klopfer, 2008). Technology-enriched projects with which I've been associated include fifth graders studying water quality in a local creek and mapping how the water quality changes with changes in land use (Coulter, 2000a) and students using handheld computers to investigate interdependence in the bottomland forest portion of our ecology center (Coulter, 2012). Whether the work involves modeling the community with sand and string as Mitchell described, or with the latest technology, place has a long history in education leading to its current instantiation in concepts of place-based education.

Beyond the specifically geographic dimensions of place-based learning, a broader emphasis on engaging students actively with the local environment has a similarly long history. Some of the earliest efforts to engage students with the environment as part of the school curriculum were grounded in the Nature Study movement spearheaded by Liberty Hyde Bailey, Anna Botsford Comstock, and others at Cornell University at the dawn of the 20th century. As Comstock (1986, p. 1) described it rather self-evidently, "Nature study is, despite all discussions and perversions, a study of nature." Lest we write this off as a recursive loop of the obvious, she goes on to draw a distinction between nature study as she perceives it and a more formal science-based treatment that draws kids away from a direct study of the flora and fauna in their local community:

> If we are teaching the science of ornithology, we take first the Archaeopteryx, then the scratching birds, and finally reach the song birds, studying each as part of the whole. Nature study begins with the robin because the child sees it and is interested in it, and notes things about the habits and appearance of the robin that may be perceived by intimate observation. (p. 5)

She goes on to assert that a child will over time build a sophisticated understanding of ornithology inductively from successive direct experiences with birds of interest. While this claim that students will build larger concepts simply from an accumulation of activities is debatable, the key element for our purposes is simply to show that local ecology as a focus for environmental education has a history dating back more than a hundred years. Of course, this consideration of the role of place within formal education bypasses the broader history of the human race, as children throughout time have been raised in and learned about their local culture and surroundings. It's only with the rise of the modern school that we have chosen to cut our young off from their surroundings by locking them indoors for an increasing fraction of their childhood.

While these examples reflect practice within the United States, it's important to note that this impetus to support place-based education as a concept has broad international support. Writing from the United Kingdom, Joy Palmer and Philip Neal (1994) cite a number of projects in England as well as in Australia that focus on local involvement as an educational strategy. Often described there as "field study" or "field work" projects, these community-based efforts seek to make authentic neighborhood connections to enrich a learning environment that would otherwise remain limited to textbook-style examples. The most ambitious of these projects, Palmer and Neal argue, go beyond community-based learning to encompass direct action. They describe a sequence of practice starting from teachers' efforts fostering students' enthusiasm for investigating a local issue, moving on to providing guidance as students conduct the necessary research on relevant issues, from there leading to the selection of an action plan, and then culminating in students implementing their plan and monitoring results (Palmer & Neal, 1994). This approach largely mirrors in its values and approaches similar pedagogic frameworks labeled "service-learning" (National Youth Leadership Council, 2008) and "action competence" (Jensen, 2004; Jensen & Schnack, 1997). We'll be considering the merit of these approaches in the next chapter.

Looking further afield, Hart (1997) describes a wide range of projects in which students in developing countries both learn and take action to benefit their communities. Noting that many areas are experiencing increasing urbanization, Hart cites a number of cases in which traditional indigenous knowledge is being replaced with less culturally and ecologically connected learning, leading to a need to revitalize connections to place. For example, a program in the Brazilian Amazon helps children learn basics like the natural resources found in the community and their nutritional benefits. In Columbia, Hart documents a school where there are a number of environmental projects happening simultaneously, each managed by a committee of students elected from each grade in the school. For example, Hart notes that at the time of his writing the worm farm committee was headed by a 9-year-old. Rather than separating the school from the community and assuming that kids aren't competent until they graduate (if then), it is an expectation at this school that young students are actively involved, talking with the community about issues they are concerned about—even if it means challenging adults to change their behaviors.

Projects such as these offer an alternative to the separation of school from the community that most readers will be familiar with. As Dewey (1902/1990) expressed it long ago in his classic *School and Society*,

> Through [active community projects] the entire spirit of the school is renewed. It has a chance to affiliate itself with life, to become the child's habitat, where he learns through directed living, instead of only being a place to learn lessons having an abstract and remote reference to some possible living to be done in the future. (p. 18)

Giving a bit more form to this active involvement, Hart (1997) formulated a "ladder of participation" describing increasing levels of student ownership of their work. At the lower level, he discards token or symbolic forms of involvement as "non-participation" while giving higher status to projects in which youth take real responsibility for guiding the direction of the effort. We'll take a closer look at the ladder in Chapter 2 as we analyze student ownership of their work.

As should be clear by now, place-based education builds on a long and geographically widespread tradition worthy of consideration as we seek to create improved environmental learning opportunities for students. While referring specifically to his work in Australia, Steve Malcolm (1990, as cited in Palmer & Neal 1994, p. 96) encapsulates quite nicely the value of place-based education as it might be undertaken in any culture when he remarks that "it is vital to recognize that actively involved people generally undergo far greater development of abilities, understanding, and environmental commitment for the future than do passive receivers of information or those who theorize but do not act." These outcomes speak well to place-based education being a constructive means of addressing contemporary concerns such as people's increasing disconnection with the natural world, the sterility of much of today's "do not touch" approach to environmental education, and developmental concerns about the appropriateness of young children being exposed to crisis-based environmental education.

In his best-selling work *Last Child in the Woods*, Richard Louv (2005) famously coined the term "nature deficit disorder" (p. 99). While he never meant for it to be taken as a medical diagnosis, he does suggest that greater exposure to nature might be an effective response to current concerns such as Attention-Deficit Hyperactivity Disorder (ADHD). More generally, Louv (2005) describes features of modern childhood that may be contributing to changes in young people's behaviors:

> As recently as the 1950s, most families still had some kind of agricultural connection. Many of these children, girls as well as boys, would have been directing their energy and physicality in constructive ways: doing farm chores, baling hay, splashing in the swimming hole, climbing trees, racing to the sandlot for a game of baseball. Their unregimented play would have been steeped in nature. (p. 101)

Today, of course, it is rare that kids have this level of unstructured, unsupervised time. Instead, the range of free play is greatly circumscribed. Robert Krulwich (2012) cites the case of several generations of a British family in which the range of allowed play ranged from 6 miles away from home for an 8-year-old back in 1919, down to a mile in 1950, half a mile in the late 1970s, and now just to the end of the street. Lest we think this evolution toward restrictions on kids' movement is idiosyncratic to that particular family or a feature solely of the current generation of children, Hillman, Adams, and Whitelegg (1990) reported on a study investigating children's mobility in Great Britain and Germany in the 1970s and 1980s. In both cultures, they found significantly more restrictions on free movements, owing largely to growing concerns about dangers from increased levels of traffic and more awareness of the risk of child molestation.

Clearly, over time there has been a broad trend toward restricting young people's free access to nature. In my own experience talking with parent groups, they recognize this as a problem and see clearly the limits on experience that restrictions impose. Despite this, by and large they are unwilling for their child to take the risk and become "a statistic." The extent to which this conservatism toward children's space has become the norm was reflected in the outcry against Lenore Skenazy when she sent her 9-year-old son home by himself on the New York City subway. In her book *Free-Range Kids*, Skenazy (2010) shares an adventure in parenting that exhibits a level of trust and confidence that is distinctively uncommon today. While we can—and should—bemoan this loss of kids' freedom and cite reasons for more open-ended time in nature, we can also mitigate the limits placed on young people's outdoor engagement. While not a substitute for free and unstructured play, place-based educational projects do provide sustained, meaningful outdoor experiences that they likely wouldn't have otherwise.

The level of community engagement offered by a strong place-based education program also serves to counter the trend toward "hands-off" approaches to environmental education. As David Sobel (2012) notes ruefully:

> Much of environmental education today has taken on a museum mentality, where nature is a composed exhibit on the other side of the glass. Children can look at it and study it, but they can't do anything with it. The message is: Nature is fragile. Look, but don't touch. Ironically, this "take only photographs, leave only footprints" mindset crops up in the policies and programs of many organizations trying to preserve the natural world and cultivate children's relationships to it. (para. 16)

There certainly are places where there ought to be a distance kept, whether because the setting is in fact intended for display or for real reasons of safety (which is not the same as a lawyer-driven paranoia of what might happen). For example, like most botanical gardens, the main campus of my employer—the Missouri Botanical Garden—is explicitly a horticultural display space. Still, it's a great place for teachers and kids to observe a range of special plants, many of which don't grow locally. Because of this extra level of care required for some plants and the more general focus on ornamental display, there is a "hands-off" policy. Just as you don't finger the paintings in an art museum, these are plants to be seen and not touched. Even with this limitation, museum-like natural experiences can be incredibly valuable as a learning resource. When I was teaching elementary school science full-time, I took my fourth grade kids to the botanical garden as an extension of field research that we were conducting in a local forest. Our time in the garden's Climatron provided a chance for the kids to compare and contrast Missouri woodland plants with those that could be found in a tropical rainforest. Through this experience, critically important environmental concepts were reinforced as students saw how certain adaptations like drip-tip leaves helped plants survive in environments with high levels of precipitation. In terms of learning potential, this first-hand observation within a display-only environment was much better than watching a video on the rainforest.

Still, as educators we need to remember that these exceptional cases don't justify the sweeping trend toward banning direct contact with nature. Research summarized by Louise Chawla (2009) shows the importance of first-hand engagement, not distant viewing, as being critical in helping people become what she terms "an agent of care for the natural world." To support this growth process, natural sites need to welcome active, hands-on exploration that fosters deep engagement with nature. While we don't want to encourage wanton destruction, we also need to recognize that nature is resilient. The guideline we give our volunteers who lead groups of kids at the Litzsinger Road Ecology Center is simply to notice their surroundings: If a leaf or flower is plentiful, picking a few won't hurt. From a safety point of view, rolling down a hill or scrabbling back up a creek bank after skipping stones is a healthy way to enjoy being in nature. Dirty pants and an occasional scrape are just part of the experience. These nature bonding experiences, coupled with meaningful projects that foster a kid's sense of agency toward the environment, will help build an ethic of care and respect that is much more robust than a reverential but ultimately distancing "hands-off" approach. Look, touch, feel, care, and act need to be our guiding principles.

Another angle on distancing kids from the environment is also worth exploring. Aside from keeping kids from touching the environment, there is also a tendency to make "the environment" something exotic and geographically far away. Compounding the distance issue, when we focus on big global concerns prematurely we make the environment a scary and ultimately depressing place, which can contribute to a psychic distance from nature. Whereas previous generations of kids had to deal with the threat of nuclear warfare, we saddle the present generation with dire environmental prophecies of deforestation and global warming that will bring untold catastrophe to the world. While we shouldn't diminish real global environmental concerns, it's also important that we don't expect our 8-year-olds to solve them. As David Sobel (1996) advises, kids should not be engaged in large-scale environmental tragedies at an early age. Instead, we need to focus on locally scaled projects that engage kids at the right developmental level and that are responsive to their initiatives. These projects offer a much more promising place to start.

The legacy of progressive approaches to education—in particular John Dewey's conception of experience, to which we turn next—offers guidance in making curriculum choices that resonate at just the right place with the students involved. The chapters ahead will unpack the complexities involved, but as a general principle, local efforts are the best place to start since they have the benefit of being anchored in the community where the kids live. As a result, there is a potential for first-hand experience from which to draw, as well as the opportunity to have this experience grow in richness and complexity through sustained engagement. Along with the locality, scale is also important to ensure that it's a problem the kids can wrap their heads around, and that they can feel they have made a difference. The role of meaningful action can't be understated. Reading about the plight of an endangered species and holding a bake sale to send money to help avert a far-off environmental tragedy reinforces a model of nature as a distant phenomenon "out there." It's also a bit too easy to put a stamp on it and be done. Instead, if we want kids to become the agents of care that Chawla describes, then they need to roll up their sleeves and get dirty.

Exploring the Underpinnings of Experience

Before we roll up our mental sleeves and get dirty analyzing the opportunities and challenges involved in place-based education, it's important to invest just a few minutes in exploring its philosophical underpinnings. As we will see, the choice to move toward supporting kids in significant community engagement is more profound and meaningful than simply adopting a new program model. Instead, the choice calls up fundamental aspects of teachers' personal and professional identity, and in turn helps to sculpt participating youths' emerging sense of themselves. Given this gravity, we need to be sure our own understanding is sufficiently grounded so that we can appreciate more fully the challenges and opportunities described in the pages ahead.

If we had to categorize place-based education within the spectrum of educational philosophies, it would fall by and large within the progressive strand. As noted before, an in-depth look at progressive education is beyond the scope of the book. Still, we need one more peek to make sense of what follows in the balance of the book. While it is easy to reduce progressive education to a caricature of a laissez-faire "do what you want" sort of approach to learning,[1] serious studies of progressive education (e.g., Dewey, 1938a/1963; Lowe, 2007; Nager & Shapiro, 2000) show that it can be a very intentional, value-driven approach that leads to productive learning.

---

[1] See, for example, the caricature of progressive education in the novel *Fin & Lady* by Cathleen Schine (2013). In it, the 11-year-old protagonist is growing up in Greenwich Village in the '60s, attending the New Flower School. While there, Fin's language lessons are characterized as fluffy activities such as reading liner notes from Bob Dylan albums and arranging colored blocks for math lessons.

For our purposes, two of the more significant points of contrast between traditional and progressive approaches are to be found in the scope of content to be covered, and the nature of students' engagement with that content. A traditional school will usually have a number of pre-specified units to be covered, most often guided by a textbook or textbook-like materials that provide the scripting for the instruction. Contrasting this, a progressive approach most often has fewer curriculum focal points pursued in more depth, anchored in more authentic materials. Trade books and field guides fill the bookshelves, and tools for measurement and observation populate the classroom. To be more specific, real tools. Thus, for example, students in a well-developed progressive school will use magnifying glasses (not disposable plastic substitutes) and balance scales that are accurate enough to allow meaningful comparisons. Emphasis is on doing real work in ways that are appropriate for the age, not a simulation of work. Throughout, there is a privileging of depth over breadth, and of respect for the kids as increasingly autonomous, self-driven learners. As Dewey (1938a/1963) argues:

> To imposition from above is opposed expression and cultivation of individuality; to external discipline is opposed free activity; to learning from texts and teachers, learning through experience; to acquisition of isolated skills and techniques by drill, is opposed acquisition of them as a means of attaining ends which make direct vital appeal; to preparation for a more or less remote future is opposed making the most of the opportunities of the present life; to static aims and materials is opposed acquaintance with a changing world. (p. 19)

If we are to engage in place-based education as a pedagogic strategy, I will go so far as to argue that progressive values such as these are essential. In fact, perhaps the most concise set of guidelines for place-based learning is offered by Dewey (1938a/1963) in *Experience and Education*, his last major statement on education (and from which the previous quote was drawn). Anyone contemplating designing a place-based project would be well advised to read this short volume as a primer. Specifically, Dewey offers four cornerstone concepts that support a well-designed project: continuity, interaction, purpose, and progressive organization of subject matter. Given their foundational nature, it's worth spending time looking at each in turn to see how they help to sculpt what Dewey (1938a/1963) would call "a correct idea of experience" (p. 20). To that end, he correctly points out that some experiences can be what he terms "miseducative" (p. 10) if in fact they serve to stunt future learning and growth. For example, if chaotic sequencing of learning experiences impairs sense-making, or if an unengaging learning environment breeds passivity among students, these are miseducative experiences. Hence he delineates the four criteria as guideposts.

By continuity, Dewey is advocating for an intentional linking of what has gone before and what comes after. As he notes (1938a/1963, p. 35), "The principle of continuity of experience means that every experience both takes up something from those [experiences] which have gone before and modifies in some way the quality of those which come after." This principle directly challenges a transmission model wherein the primary concern is simply that the units of understanding be delivered. This happens all too often in modern education. Taken to an extreme, it doesn't even matter who does the delivery. For example, in some elementary grades colleagues divide up the science units they are required to "cover," with teachers repeating their assigned unit to each of the classes in a six- to eight-week rotation. Each child engages with the units with their classmates but in an idiosyncratic manner. One class might have the units in an A-B-C-D sequence, while another might have a D-C-B-A sequence, and so on. Aside from the lack of continuity in experience—since it will be infinitely harder for each experience to build on what has gone before and feed what is coming up—a child in this environment has a "teacher continuity" problem. With a new science teacher every couple of months, who is keeping tabs on the child's growing interests and dispositions?

Paired with continuity, Dewey suggests rich interaction as an essential criterion for an educative experience. Here he is stating that a learner needs to have dynamic interactions with the environment in which he or she is working. This might include the social environment, with meaningful interactions with peers, the teacher, and other adults in the community. It might also involve thoughtful interaction with materials so that productive learning occurs. Looking back at the project examples at the start of this chapter, the fifth graders developing a native plant garden had extended interactions with their teacher and one of my staff members, as well as with print and online resources that were essential for reaching a goal they valued: having a well-designed garden that would enhance their school yard.

This emphasis on interaction, considered in multiple dimensions, has been a staple of more progressive approaches to education. It has been most well articulated perhaps in the "developmental-interaction approach" that has been foundational to the Bank Street College of Education, both in its teacher education programs and in its laboratory school for preschool and elementary school students. At the risk of oversimplification, a developmental-interactionist would argue that the life of the mind is important, but that it is enriched considerably by the extent to which a learner interacts with adults, peers, and materials. In describing the roots of the developmental-interaction approach, Shapiro and Biber (1972) draw strong similarities to the cognitive work of Piaget and others, but they enhance this perspective with a much greater focus on the environment in which people learn. They remark:

> It is a basic tenet of the developmental-interaction approach that the growth of cognitive functions—acquiring and ordering information, judging, reasoning, problem solving, using systems of symbols—cannot be separated from the growth of personal

and interpersonal processes—the development of self-esteem and a sense of identity, internalization of impulse control, capacity for autonomous response, relatedness to other people. The interdependence of these developmental processes is the sine qua non of the developmental-interaction approach. (p. 61)

Thus, a critical distinction can be drawn between developmental-interaction approaches and traditional academically focused classrooms in the extent to which the more fully integrated developmental-interaction approach values both the affective and cognitive domains of learning.

The level of interaction in which the student engages feeds into Dewey's third criterion: that the students have a purpose to guide their work. To be clear here, a purpose in this context is an internally felt one, whether it be the pre-teen garden designers looking to have a well-thought-out plan, or the middle school tornado mappers looking to make sense of a path of overwhelming destruction within a mile or so of their school. In either case, there is a level of self-direction that is critical in discerning whether a sense of purpose is held by the students, or whether they are responding to external prompts. Whether it's jumping like a trained seal for treats like extra recess for good behavior, or recoiling from threats, reactive direction can't be considered a purpose in discerning the educative value of an experience. Even in a more benign context, students who are nominally free to pursue their work aren't really engaged in purposeful behavior if they are just checking off tasks assigned by the teacher. Piecework is no more personally fulfilling in fourth grade than it is on a factory floor.

Rather, a student needs to be working toward a sense of autonomy, relatedness to others, and personal competence—the three key elements of self-determination theory (Deci & Ryan, 2002) that align so well with Dewey's articulation of purpose. Viewed specifically within an educational context, Reeve (2002) summarizes a wide range of research findings indicating that "students achieve highly, learn conceptually, and stay in school in part because their teachers support their autonomy rather than control their behavior" (p. 183). Going further, Reeve identifies specific behaviors shown by these autonomy-supporting teachers (ranging from the trust they have in students being able to solve problems to more mundane things like how closely they hold on to instructional materials rather than passing them along to their students). Resulting behaviors and emotions from students include factors critical to place-based education including greater attention, effort, participation, and persistence, as well as greater interest, enjoyment, enthusiasm, and a lack of anxiety or anger (Reeve, 2002). Collectively, these cognitive and non-cognitive factors reflect a level of purposeful engagement that runs counter to the passive disengagement too many students exhibit.

Closing the set of four principles, Dewey advocates for a progressive organization of subject matter that supports a student's unfolding of understanding and capacity. For example, one school I work with that has a growing commitment to place-based education has articulated a nice sequence for their second through fourth graders. The second graders spend a good bit of time investigating the basic ecology of their back yard, school yard, and the grounds at our ecology center. Key concepts here include signs of seasonal change, plant and animal interaction, and the like. For a research project on growing conditions, they collect soil samples from the different habitats at our center (which can vary quite a bit from the silty soil in much of the floodplain to the gravelly soil closer to the road running past the center). In third grade, the kids develop these basic ecological understandings further as they take moral ownership of the reconstructed prairie being developed on the school grounds. It becomes their space for the year, to tend and care for. The ecological impact of a strong habitat becomes the focus in fourth grade, as students take responsibility for a bird garden, which is a new habitat now being developed on the school grounds. Here, the plant–animal interactions are more overt and thus central to the students' emerging understanding of local ecology. Note the successively complex concepts the students are engaging with, supported by a progressive organization of subject matter. We're currently working with the building principal and faculty to look at extending this chain to grades above and below this three-grade arc. Later in the book we'll compare this model of intentional sequencing with another that by design made essentially random assignment of unit sequences from year to year. In that district, at least at the time, when you learned something depended on which year in the curriculum cycle you were born in.

In sum, Dewey offers us four simple yet profound ideas: that one experience should draw from and feed the next; that learning is best supported by a rich interaction with people and materials; that internal purposes and drive are essential in motivating learning; and that subject matter should build progressively in its scope and complexity. These four foundational concepts can in turn be translated into specific goals for the design of learning environments. Offered by Shapiro and Biber (1972, pp. 62–63) for younger children, they arguably apply to all learning environments:

1. To strengthen the commitment to and pleasure in work and learning
2. To broaden and deepen sensitivity to experience
3. To promote cognitive power and intellectual mastery
4. To support the integration of affective and cognitive domains
5. To nurture self-esteem and self-understanding
6. To encourage differentiated interaction with people
7. To promote the capacity to participate in a social order in the classroom and in the school

Clearly these design principles build on Dewey's emphasis on continuity, interaction, purpose, and progressive organization of subject matter, and are at work in place-based education programs such as the ones captured in the vignettes that open the chapter and in other examples we will analyze in the pages ahead. Whether you are a 10-year-old advancing your understanding of botany as you design and build a garden that will be noticed by your peers, parents, and others, or you are a young teen building an identity that includes learning how to use advanced technologies to understand a recent natural disaster in your community, you are actively learning, not just fluffing through a caricatured progressive education or being carried along the path of a traditional curriculum. There is much more at stake, driven by a higher level of engagement.

This harkening back to a progressive legacy isn't meant to be a trip down memory lane or a wish to return to old-time values. If anything, the progressive paradigm has never had a sustained period of dominance in schools. In the United States, progressive reforms have tended to cluster in schools (often private schools, at that) that are arranged for that purpose, or in schools that thrived under the personal leadership of educators with a progressive bent. Even in the British context, the primary schools that were for a time the exemplar of progressive education have been by and large reduced to an increasingly standardized, academically focused venture (Lowe, 2007). Perhaps the most promising alternative to standardized, delivery-focused education today is found in Finland (Ripley, 2013; Sahlberg, 2011). There, most of the dominant logic of Western schooling has been stood on its head—for instance, there is less time spent in school, less homework is given, and teachers have greater autonomy—with results that place Finnish schools at or near the top in the same international comparisons that motivate American schools to double down and focus even more intently on the robotic transmission model that gives us middling results.

Progressive Educational Values Today

If we can avoid the caricatured notions of progressive education, it is clear that the legacy described here is relevant to place-based education and other initiatives that depend on active student engagement. This painting of a historical portrait is not intended to suggest that all of the wisdom resides in the past. Rather, through a continual updating based on new insights, the tradition continues to grow and evolve. This should not be surprising, since an underlying premise of Dewey's pragmatic approach was one of active experimentation and valuing of ideas for their outcomes, not a worshipping of tenets simply by how longstanding they are. Similarly, in reflecting on the developmental-interaction approach, Shapiro and Biber (1972) attest to the vitality of the model as they close their essay by noting:

> It is to be hoped that what may emerge from research on these problems is a sharpened theoretical understanding of the interaction of social forms with dynamic processes of development and a more effective roster of educational techniques. The developmental-interaction approach, like all theoretical structures, must be ready to accommodate its principles and practices to such information. (p. 79)

Thus, progressive education as a paradigm benefits from continuing research such as efforts by Martin (2000) to integrate aspects of social learning described by Vygotsky into the developmental-interaction approach, and work to infuse teacher education programs with these values (Pignatelli, 2000).

One modern strand worth considering in this effort to continue growing and renewing the progressive legacy is the work currently being done to promote intellectual and participatory virtues in education. Together, these bodies of work are updating long-standing concern for learners' ongoing growth and engagement. For the intellectual virtues, Jason Baehr (2013) has articulated a set of interrelated traits including "curiosity, open-mindedness, attentiveness, intellectual carefulness, intellectual courage, intellectual rigour, and intellectual honesty" (p. 248). Speaking from a philosophical point of view, Baehr goes on to argue that one acts on these virtues out of "a love of epistemic goods . . . like knowledge, truth and understanding" (p. 248). While I'm not aware of any explicit connection Baehr makes to education for community engagement in the sense we are using it, he does offer a directly related argument in noting how acting on these intellectual virtues reflects a very personal level of engagement. Bridging the gap to place-based education, the intellectual virtues he lists clearly reflect the dispositions and actions that are characteristic of a student bringing her best thinking to community problems. Conversely, it is hard to imagine a student exhibiting these intellectual virtues in a more passive school environment that didn't reflect Dewey's parameters of continuity of experience in school with the rest of life, rich interaction with the cultural and physical environment, a vigorous and internally felt sense of purpose, and progressively complex organization of subject matter. Specific to the idea of intellectual virtue being propelled by purpose, Baehr notes that in acting on a virtue, "one has good reason to think it will be useful in achieving one's epistemic ends" (p. 250) and that doing so exhibits dimensions of a person's competence and rationality. In sum, considerations of intellectual virtues such as those offered by Baehr provide a typology of sorts to the kinds of thinking that take place in what Dewey (1938a/1963) would term an educative environment.

Building on this, Pritchard (2013) offers an analysis of cognitive agency, or the ability to use capacities such as those offered by Baehr (2013) to build understanding. Thus, instead of taking knowledge as received, a person exhibiting some level of cognitive agency is bringing active thinking to bear on the problem, either to tease out a solution or at least to verify its accuracy. Pritchard offers a simple example contrasting a child who looks up a mathematical "fact" such as the square root of 9 and a child who is in a position to understand how this answer was arrived at, and—I would add—perhaps even have the depth of knowledge to understand why there is more than one possible answer.[2] The exercise of this cognitive agency through owning the learning process is a critical point of differentiation from a model of received knowledge. Looking specifically at environmental learning, a similar contrast could be made between a student who nominally "knows" the ecoregion he lives in and one who can use the mesh of understandings that go with that. Thus, when we work with teachers and students on building up gardens with Missouri native plants, their knowing or being willing to research characteristic features like how the temperature and precipitation typical of the region favor some plants over others helps in making the garden a "thought-full" endeavor. On a more local scale, factors such as availability of sunlight, soil types, and access to water help in making garden design decisions. The net result is a difference in level of engagement reflecting variation in levels of cognitive agency. Pritchard (2013) captures this contrast by analogy when he observes that:

> Watson may see the dirt on the subject's shoe, and so come to know that her shoes are unpolished (mere cognitive achievement), whereas Sherlock will immediately observe much more than this, seeing straight away, perhaps, that the subject before him lacks an alibi for the murder (strong cognitive achievement). (p. 240)

In sum, capacities reflecting intellectual virtue and cognitive agency are important and arguably essential dimensions of what it means to be educated. They certainly are critical in a place-based environment wherein the issues are real and often messy, not simplified for textbook analysis. Rather, a fairly sophisticated level of cognitive agency on the part of the teacher and student will be called upon if they are to make sense of the issues and to devise an action plan.

One more contemporary progressive construct relevant for our analysis is the idea of participatory virtues. Matt Ferkany and Kyle Powys Whyte (2011) begin by describing these as "virtues enabling inclusiveness and engagement with the harder things" (p. 333). Going further, they argue that there are less obvious cognitive and epistemic benefits when people demonstrate these virtues. As an example, they discuss ways in which self-confident people have the poise needed to work through complex information that might challenge preconceptions, work competently with authorities, and (assuming that one's self-confidence doesn't inflate to the point at which it becomes willful pride) not be invested in being right so much as working toward the best answer. Else-

---

[2] For those brushing up on their math skills, squaring either 3 or -3 gives you 9.

where Ferkany and Whyte (2012) show how reasonableness represents virtuous behavior as it takes into account others' needs and interests beyond what accrues to one's own benefit. This way of being is contrasted with a purely rational perspective such as that offered by classical economics in which people seek to maximize self-interest.

Based on their analysis, Ferkany and Whyte (2012) offer a list of 14 virtues that are relevant for one or more of the key purposes they identify (inclusiveness, engagement, or epistemic productivity): wit, friendliness, empathy and charity, courage, temperance, sincerity, humility, basic self-confidence, resilience and persistence, attentiveness, dependability, reasonableness and fairness, generosity, and patience. Similar to the ways in which intellectual virtues and cognitive agency give a guide to the capacities needed for place-based education projects, participatory virtues also help to ensure successful learning. Since authentic place-based problems are rarely "cut and dried" either in the framing of the issues or in defining the best path forward, the multiplicity of perspectives and commitment to collaborative inquiry fostered through participatory virtues can be invaluable. Looking at ways to develop these capacities in students, Ferkany and White (2011) implicitly endorse approaches like place-based education as they advocate for "learning models in which knowledge is not merely received passively, but is reconstructed in the learner through experience, active engagement with the subject matter, and dialogic inquiry with others" (p. 337).

Returning to our analysis of the challenges and opportunities of place-based education, these progressive ideas have direct bearing on the issues at hand. Much more than simply adding a field trip or two to liven up a class, full engagement in the community builds from a distinctive way of seeing the educational endeavor. As Smith (2013) summarizes it:

> One of the central aims of place-based education is to enlist the intelligence, energy, and skills of young people in the process of community and environmental revitalization and restoration. The hope is that by inviting students into this work, they will find reasons to learn and that the social and natural communities that surround them will become both healthier and more sustainable as a result of their involvement. (p. 219)

While we may be excited at the prospect of rich experiences that account for factors such as continuity, interaction, and purpose, we need to note at the outset that this type of engagement is diametrically counter to the role expectations held by most teachers and the larger school systems they function within. This single factor may go a long way in explaining the gap in teachers' ability and disposition to lead intensive, community-based projects with their students. A traditionally focused teacher viewing design principles such as those just cited from Shapiro and Biber (1972) may see components like "pleasure in work and learning" and the "integration of affective and cognitive domains" and decide that these are well and good if they can be accomplished, but that the kids need to be prepared for the end-of-year tests or next grade or some other upcoming eventuality. Somewhere in the logic of mainstream schooling, Dewey's dictum about education being life, not a preparation for life, gets lost. Testing, pacing charts, and even the underlying teacher–student logic of "I teach, you do" work against the progressive values laid out over the course of this chapter.

As a teacher, administrator, or school board member, if your vision of how a "good teacher" functions doesn't encompass an active role for students, or if accountability structures work against this approach, it will be hard to teach this way. This is what makes successful place-based teaching a heroic endeavor. Even if you can nominally support high levels of student ownership and engagement, it will be in a sense foreign to you if these values aren't central to your pedagogic vision. Recall that the initial gap in teacher practice that gave rise to this analysis was in an after-school setting in which there were no pacing or testing accountability measures in place. Where we thought the freedom would be liberating, it proved to be so only for some of the teachers. Others didn't experience (or at least, didn't act on) the freedom given. Chapters 3 and 4 will explore these professional choices and trade-offs in some depth. I'll be arguing that it is precisely this "values and vision gap" between progressive and traditional education that leads to some teachers being able to implement rich place-based programs whereas others struggle. Toward the end of the book we'll look at the potential for addressing this gap to create more meaningful and engaged learning experiences for everyone. But first, we need to lay more groundwork in Chapter 2 by looking at how students engage in place-based projects that embody the progressive values just described.

Fledging Students to Be Active Agents in the World

I n this chapter, we'll take a look at how students experience programs that actively work to develop their character, competence, and sense of place. As we do this, we will see the progressive principles described in the last chapter at work in real settings, in school and out. Far from scripted compliance, the teachers and students we will meet are active agents, pursuing important goals. In addition to clarifying the contrast with traditional norms of schooling, this chapter lays the groundwork for the analysis of teachers' design choices that will be taken up in Chapters 3 and 4. As we will see throughout the rest of the book, choices made by teachers in how to structure the classroom and how to use materials lead to different student experiences, even if the teachers are working from nominally the same curriculum materials. In turn, kids' experiences of learning and of themselves become radically different.

Recall the discussion in the Preface about how underlying frameworks drive both our worldview and how we engage in experiences. This is no less true for kids than it is for teachers. If students come to see school as a passive activity to be engaged with simply to minimize friction within the school or at home, they will take on the "robot" role Mills (1959/2000) described, though the cheerfulness aspect may not be there. Where students find value in a passive environment, it tends to be placed on securing external, immediate gratification rewards such as the student whose highlight of the year-long LIONS program was that "it was really fun when we got candy every time we got a question [right]." We have found that if students can instead be placed in a dynamic and engaging context, they can liven up to become thoughtful participants. Contrast the candy-driven student with a student across town in a more active program whose most valued experience was the much more adventurous and internally driven process of learning "how to make a house in [Google] SketchUp" that was part of a larger effort by her group to craft a vision of their city 25 years in the future.

This assumption of an active role by the students is essential, since an underlying goal for many place-based projects is that they not only understand critical dimensions of local history, culture, and environment, but also that they are able to take some significant action that improves local conditions. So, for example, a class studying a local stream may want to take on water-quality improvement projects through a community education effort or perhaps through a planting project to mitigate stream bank erosion. A class concerned about the impact of declining pollinator populations might want to design and build a native plant garden in their school yard. The key difference here between a fully articulated place-based project and a simple field trip is in the focus of the effort. A typical field trip is designed to get students out of the classroom to gain some level of experience with an issue or a location first-hand. By itself, this is not a bad outcome in that it makes whatever is being explored more real than if it were represented solely by a textbook, video, or online resource. A place-based project worthy of its name goes well beyond that to focus on full engagement. Minimally, it represents a sustained effort to investigate a local place or event in some depth. Ideally it goes even further, supporting students in taking meaningful action. Each of the examples of place-based practice cited in this book includes at least some degree of action that allows students to take on the identity of a citizen in the community. Through this type of project, students are motivated by more than a grade or a piece of candy. Rather, there is an authentic, real-world concern animating the students' efforts, which requires a fully active human presence. Successful engagement draws on (and nurtures growth in) students' cognitive and emotional capacities in ways that a one-off field trip largely cannot. Unless it is very tightly tied to the learning goals and the overall flow of inquiry in the classroom, a single field trip just can't achieve the level of focused engagement made possible by an extended project.

If we accept this premise, what should a good project look like? How can a teacher orchestrate such a complex endeavor? For some teachers designing the classroom environment to support this intensive engagement is simply intuitive, coming naturally out of their commitment to making learning meaningful for their students. Others build this level of involvement by framing it as a component of a formal service-learning program. Whether it is done intuitively or as part of a structured process, the addition of a service-learning component to a curriculum is a very useful enhancement. Following recommended practices for service-learning from the National Youth Leadership Council (2008) ensures that participating students have:

- Meaningful service opportunities
- Links to the required curriculum or other program goals
- Opportunities for reflection on the experience

- Programs that reflect and build respect for diversity
- Opportunities for youth to develop their voice
- Partnerships with relevant organizations
- Structured opportunities to monitor progress
- Programs with sufficient duration and intensity

It is hard to argue with these as valued educational outcomes. All else being equal, it is certainly a curricular improvement for students to go beyond solely academic learning and engage with real-world contexts for what they are studying. Inevitably, students participating in a project will absorb on site a great deal of relevant tacit knowledge that their texts and other curriculum materials didn't convey. If they are also conducting activities as part of their service-learning efforts, they can deepen underlying skills such as measurement and data recording through the practice afforded by the experience. Also, as just noted, the motivational benefits of making a difference are important for students' identity development. These benefits are all to the good and not to be passed over lightly.

Service-learning as a curricular framing device, however, has some limitations that need to be considered. Foremost among these is its persistent confusion with notions of community service, often built in as a school graduation requirement or as a court-mandated restitution for the commission of minor crimes. Clearly, we (and most advocates of service-learning as it is described here) are after something more than that. Unfortunately, the mixed meanings create a connotation of simple activities like litter pickups and stream cleaning as "service-learning." Even if we resolve the linguistic confusion, service-learning as a concept can still be unnecessarily limiting. Yes, students should be involved in the community, and they should have opportunities reflecting the principles listed above. Efforts to embed service-learning opportunities as part of students' educational programs are important and valuable as far as they go. But, do they go far enough? The standards listed above assume that effective service-learning provides opportunities to apply "knowledge and skills" (p. 1) and address "issues that are personally relevant to the participants" (p. 1). Again, these are undoubtedly good areas of focus, but there is no assumption explicitly embedded in the standards that the youth are positioned for ownership. Instead service-learning simply "involves youth in the decision-making process" (p. 3). As we will see shortly, this level of engagement is only mid-range in the spectrum of possibilities.

Thus, while service-learning taken in an active sense can (and often does) motivate great learning opportunities, it also has the potential to create only a modicum of engagement, which doesn't sufficiently shift the learning dynamic. Instead, effective environmental education needs to assume and articulate at least a trajectory toward more advanced levels of student ownership, even if the students aren't yet ready to achieve that level of participation. The goal should be, as Schusler, Krasny, Peters, and Decker (2009) note, "genuine participation, [where] youth take part in making meaning of a particular environmental problem by defining it, analyzing its root causes, and envisioning and enacting possible solutions" (p. 112). Service-learning as described in the National Youth Leadership Council standards opens the door for this level of participation, but leaves an ambiguity around "involvement" that is worth defining further. Even if many students won't get there in their school programs, we need to communicate the trajectory toward ownership as clearly as possible.

At the risk of getting bogged down in semantics, perhaps a useful reframing device is the more ambitious concept of action competence, advanced by Danish researchers Bjarne Jensen and Karsten Schnack among others. Phrased most succinctly, action competence involves students developing the ability to choose and take actions that have clearly intended outcomes that benefit a defined situation. When compared with service-learning, this formulation puts more emphasis on youth intention, ownership, and action, which are at best implied with the term "involvement" in the NYLC standards. However, by this enhanced level of engagement, action competence embeds several profound challenges for the design of learning experiences. As Jensen and Schnack (1997) note:

> [T]here is a need for a form of teaching from which pupils acquire the courage, commitment, and desire to get involved in the social interests concerning [the environment] (naturally based on understanding and insight). They have to learn to be active citizens in a democratic society. (p. 164)

If this is to happen, teaching for action competence has a dual focus: to build commitment to a cause and to help students develop the knowledge structures required to actually understand what is happening and how changes might have a beneficial impact. Beyond factual knowledge, students need a systems view that helps them project how an intervention for good or bad has an impact. In this way, efforts to develop action competence require a wider range of focus so that commitment and understanding become mutually reinforcing. Without this systems view, students will be ill equipped to choose meaningful and beneficial actions. Thin coverage of a wide range of topics pursued solely for their academic merit—even if the work is enhanced by application within the community—simply isn't adequate to the task. While working toward action competence as a teaching strategy is more ambitious and more demanding of teachers and students, it is arguably required for full participation in community issues.

Following on this call for refocusing our planning efforts toward a deeper and more integrated engagement, Jensen and Schnack (1997) describe two educational design issues, each of which is needed to keep the focus on the larger and more encompassing educational aspects of the project and not let the work spin off into a boot camp for environmental activists. First, the choices made about how and when to engage with the environment must be educationally driven, not based on an assumption that kids will save the world on behalf of wayward adults. The goal has to be what the kids learn and the capacities they are building for their next project, not on expanding the scope of environmental improvements. A modest improvement that builds a well-founded sense of accomplishment today and feeds commitment and capacity for future engagement is preferable to one big "blow-out" project. Second, the work must be framed within a larger context of education for democracy and participatory engagement. As Jensen and Schnack observe (1997, p. 165), "Education for democracy is thus also socialization and qualification for the role of being a participant." While the capacities for civic engagement that students have today will be limited in comparison to those they are developing, they still need to be supported as emerging citizens within the communities they are part of. We can't just keep them in a subservient role until they are 18 and then hope they hatch as fully fledged participants in society.

In making sense of student involvement and ownership, Roger Hart's (1997) ladder of participation offers a helpful guide. Based on his review of varying degrees of student participation found in a cross-cultural array of projects, Hart developed a continuum of ways in which young people become involved. These forms of participation range from deprecated acts such as token involvement on up to higher levels of citizenship where kids and adults are collaborating as peers in the design and development of community projects:

8. Child-initiated, shared decisions with adults
7. Child-initiated and directed
6. Adult-initiated; shared decisions with children
5. Consulted and informed
4. Assigned but informed
3. Tokenism
2. Decoration
1. Manipulation

Hart characterizes the three lower levels as "non-participation" while levels 4 to 8 describe increasing levels of authentic participation. Thus, projects on the fourth rung (assigned but informed) are still largely adult-driven, but there is at least a nominal effort to inform students of the reasons they are doing what they are doing. While there may be little or no youth choice in the matter, at least there is some effort to engage the kids in the project. In the three levels Hart characterizes as non-participation, one could easily argue that the kids are being exploited for window dressing or public relations purposes. It's a safe bet that toddlers at an environmental protest don't have a sophisticated understanding of the claims on the posters they are holding.

Further up Hart's ladder of participation, students take on increasing levels of engagement and ownership as they move from consultation to shared ownership, and from there on to full youth ownership. While the juxtaposition of the two highest rungs may appear paradoxical, Hart justifies them by noting that youth working with adults as collaborative peers is actually a higher level of functioning than when youth simply do their own thing (and thus, the intergenerational venture represents a more advanced level of participation). As an example of work done at a higher level on Hart's ladder, I am working with a local church youth group that has chosen a nature focus for their project work. After scoping out the church grounds to identify possible projects they could undertake, the kids identified several possible sites for planting improvements and a variety of related projects like bird houses that would enhance the natural quality of the church grounds. Working with the church administration, we as leaders identified the most viable project site from among the candidates the kids were interested in. The youth group members then selected plants from a set of options we gave them, and they then proceeded to build the garden over the course of a few Sundays. While there were some tasks we took over that the kids could have done for themselves, the time limit imposed by meeting for only an hour a week put some practical constraints on their efforts. Still, it was a productive shared adult/child effort.

More generally, there are a number of developmental and pragmatic concerns that need to be attended to in the design and implementation of complex youth projects. While it would be great simply to declare that students should be on a high rung on Hart's ladder and thus full owners of their investigations, most simply don't yet have the capacity owing to their youth and lack of experience. Turned loose without the prerequisite experiences and skills, student-led efforts will likely fail. Still, this is the direction needed if we are to fledge capable citizens over time. Adults as the more capable actors in the community need to scaffold involvement to build capacity over time. Sadly, for all too many students, school is not about participation. Rather, it is simply a game of guessing what the teacher wants and trying to deliver it.

In my last year of full-time teaching, I was in a newly created position as the science specialist for second through fourth grades in an affluent private school. These students enjoyed many material advantages, but for the most part they were also given a curricular diet that was low in intellectual nutritional value. Rather than depth of engagement, the focus was primarily on acceleration. School pride was based on having students working two to three grade levels above their age-mates from other (implicitly less successful) schools. Trying to counter this arid emphasis on acceleration over depth, I naively asked students to simply design their own inquiry: What do you want to spend a few weeks investigating? This was in the heady early days of the Internet in the late '90s, with a seeming wealth of information just a few keystrokes away. This open-ended challenge proved to be very difficult for students who were used to a diet of assigned readings, worksheets, and craft projects. After a couple of days of planning, one student broke down crying, wailing that she didn't know what I wanted her to be interested in. Note that this was simply a shift in the ownership of the information flow within the classroom, not in the much more complex and messy realm of community-engaged projects. The upshot here is that we can't simply decree where students should be; rather, there is an artful nuance required on the part of teachers to understand what level of ownership students are ready for. In schools where the culture is supportive of action competence, a teacher will likely find that students moving up to her grade will have a suite of social and academic competencies that will be missing in a school with a nearly exclusive focus on traditional academic work.

Given this conundrum, it's worth taking a moment to think about academic and personal competencies in more depth. Academically speaking, most curriculum documents—whether at the national, regional, or local level—focus on definable sets of knowledge and skills that should be learned by the end of a particular grade. While this process of assigning grade-level expectations serves an administrative planning function, it grates against the inherently integrated nature of environmental studies.[1] Coming to know your local stream requires at minimum a sense of water chemistry, biology of life cycles, and Earth science concepts such as erosion, as well as a growing understanding of ecosystems as they are found within the riparian corridor. Beyond the science disciplines, a bit of math can help with data analysis, and reading skills help in navigating field guides. Unfortunately, as a result of the somewhat arbitrary assignment of topics to a grade level, it's hard for a teacher to support integrated learning. For example, I'm currently writing curriculum focused on helping kids understand ecoregions. The driving premise of the work is to help kids understand how the temperature and precipitation that are characteristic of a region help to determine which species can live there. In short, why will you not find a polar bear in the desert or a cactus in the rainforest? Starting with an investigation of local climate conditions and the plants and animals that thrive there, the intention is for students to apply this framework to distant regions. Unfortunately, the weather and climate components of the unit are assigned to third and fifth grade in the new Next Generation Science Standards taking hold in the United States, while the ecology and life science components are fourth grade topics. Thus, teachers who don't have the autonomy to adjust their curriculum are left holding only part of what I know from my own teaching experience (Coulter, 2000b) to be a very rich integrated learning experience.

---

[1] For that matter, chunking out the curriculum in this way also runs largely counter to how people learn, but that's a separate issue.

Moreover, the assumption that learning is simply a process of running through a sequence of concepts and skills laid out in a curriculum plan is limiting. While it would be ludicrous to argue that kids shouldn't develop age-appropriate understandings and skills, it is also shortsighted to say that this is all there is to being educated. If we are to create educative experiences in a Deweyan sense, and to build students' action competence, more than factual "knowing that" and procedural "knowing how" is needed. At minimum, four dimensions of knowledge articulated by Jensen (2004) are essential for students to act with understanding:

- Effects: What is happening?
- Causes: Why is it happening?
- Visions: Where do we want to go?
- Change strategies: How can we create the changes we want to see?

One way to address this more ambitious, integrated scope of learning is to embrace the idea advanced by Robert Lawler (Lawler & Rushby, 2013) of access over coverage. Rather than simply covering the assigned curriculum, he asks how we can give kids access to what he calls the "global knowledge inheritance" they will need to become participating members of society. Note that he is not calling for students to know a laundry list of discrete ideas like those encompassed in *Cultural Literacy* (Hirsch, 1988)—an approach to education that was popular in the 1980s. Rather, Lawler draws from his background in educational technology to envision successively complex simulations that enable kids to build more nuanced and sophisticated conceptual networks. Over time, Lawler suggests, a series of simulated experiences can serve both to enable integration and application of key ideas and to provide a base of experience for subsequent learning.

While there is certainly a role for simulations and other forms of technology in helping people engage with the "global knowledge inheritance," the underlying metaphor of increasing access through iterative engagement is more important. Lawler's key point is how each productive learning experience has value both in its own right and in its ability to lay the groundwork for the next experience to occur. This is particularly true for our concerns here, since the integrated nature of environmental projects gives kids opportunities to engage with many aspects of the global knowledge inheritance in their current inquiries. As they do this, students have opportunities to use their expanding knowledge as they develop increasingly complex understandings of environmental causes and effects, and develop visions and change strategies as they seek to address local issues.

In practice, this becomes harder with arbitrary sequences like the plans touched on in the last chapter such as the three-year curriculum cycle keyed to your birth year, or the six-week shuffles during which the kids rotate from one teacher to the next to be sure they have all covered the required units, albeit in an incoherent order. Instead, intentional alignment allows a logical flow, like at the school we work with where the second grade ecology investigations fold into the third grade prairie project, leading to the fourth grade bird garden. This iterative work enables the students to develop a widened scope of understanding as they assume increasing levels of responsibility for developing and managing their school grounds. For this to work as well as it does, the teachers need to be tuned in to the kids, focused on their growth needs, and ready themselves to be active agents. Passive teachers focused on covering the curriculum and assessing knowledge and skills using traditional measures simply do not create the same learning opportunities for their kids.

In thinking about these student actions, it's important to keep in mind the many ways in which they go beyond academic learning. By design, they are meant to lead to definable environmental change and improvement. In the case of the third graders, the action component of their curriculum is the development and ongoing management of a native plant garden that offers a better habitat for pollinators and that improves storm water runoff in their school yard. To clarify the word usage, in Jensen and Schnack's (1997) framing, actions such as these can be differentiated from mere activities by the extent to which students are involved in deciding what to do and the extent to which the work is intended to solve a problem. Thus, a simple lab experiment or field trip to go see a prairie doesn't rise to the level of an "action" in this context; rather, they are an "activity" chosen by someone else, most often the teacher in an effort to provide at least a nominal base of experience attached to textbook study. Dewey, however, would likely counter that by themselves one-off "activity" projects won't have much in the way of a longer-term educative value.

To be of use, experiences need to address issues students are wrestling with now and build on the network of experiences from which they can draw in the future. Perhaps we can say that an action is an activity wrapped with intention. To make this distinction more tangible, studying erosion is an activity; planting a bioretention area to mitigate erosion is an action. Inevitably, in scoping out an action there will be subsidiary activities that enable and lead students to take on the larger action. The critical difference is in the integration: Do the disparate activities simply provide variety from the classroom routine, or do they add up to something that is student-driven and that has the potential to be environmentally and educationally significant?

Through this framing of action competence as an intentional process that is pursued at the right developmental level for the students and within a rich base of experience, community engagement takes on a qualitatively different feel. Rather than simply learning an assortment of environmental facts and concerns with a hope of producing virtuous future citizens, or providing a respite from the classroom routine through activities such as a recycling drive or a litter pickup, students building action competence are empowered. They learn to build interests and develop skills needed to take action on their growing commitments in ways that are valued by members of the community. Linking to Dewey's articulation of the educational value of experience (1938a/1963), these actions over time become part of the accumulated base from which people draw in taking new actions. Thus, a virtuous cycle is enacted whereby students fortunate enough to have ongoing nurturance of their action competence become even more engaged and capable over time. This heightened value placed on actions over activities is given further support in other educational research. For example, Johnson, Duffin, and Murphy (2012) report on a cross section of youth projects focused on air quality, documenting heightened engagement and greater learning when students are pursuing projects with directly or indirectly measurable outcomes to their efforts.

To recap the argument to this point in the chapter, action competence requires attention to four foundational elements, each of which goes considerably beyond the scope of traditional schooling: knowledge, commitment, vision, and action-focused experiences. Brought together, these four components promote much richer levels of engagement that enable students to have deeply educative experiences that foster real growth over time. More than simply banking knowledge for recall or developing skills for use some day in the undefined future, kids with action competence can do more, and have more impact in their community. In a word, they are becoming participants, not spectators. Despite the nominally more diffuse focus on learning facts, the net result of these richer learning opportunities is a greater level of access to usable understanding, as well as a greater sense of personal agency. Moving forward, we'll dig more deeply into the full scope and benefits that come with experiences focused on building students' action competence.

Building Students' Character— The Glue That Holds It All Together

A fair question at this juncture is to ask why this matters: Wouldn't it be easier just to teach students what we think they need to know when they become adults? Anyway, isn't it really just a preference? Why is this emphasis on active community-embedded learning better than another? Ultimately, yes, it is a preference how we nurture our next generation, but it's one of the most important choices we as a society will make. A review of educational history (Kliebard, 2004) shows that our goals for schools tend to oscillate over time, fluctuating from a conservatism pointed toward control and achieving narrow ends at some points, followed by comparative liberalism at other times. Since education is ultimately a public function, it's not surprising that it reflects larger social hopes and concerns. Viewed from the vantage point of the early 21st century, the United States and other Western nations are gripped with concerns about ensuring national competitiveness in a global marketplace and responding to a range of environmental concerns such as climate change. Do we focus on students' learning and preparing for an economically prosperous future, or do we take action now to save the environment? Often these concerns are portrayed as opposites. On the one hand, advocates support a robust economy, which is seen as a way to ensure good jobs and the many things that flow from this. On the other hand, others suggest that if we don't mitigate climate change, the rest won't matter. Radical changes in weather and climate patterns, as well as shifts in the cost and availability of staples like food, will be so disruptive that our sense of normal will be forever changed. The result all too often is paralysis between stereotyped corporate greed mongers and tree-huggers.

In this section and the next I will argue that it doesn't have to be an either-or decision between intellectual excellence and committed engagement. Instead I will attempt to make an affirmative defense for building students' cognitive capacities and their action competence within the context of their local communities as a preferable curriculum framing. Whether I am successful in this endeavor or not I'll leave to the reader to judge. Throughout, I will continue to echo Dewey's sagacious premise that the best way to educate for the future is to equip students to meet the challenges they face today. This runs directly counter to approaches to education that focus solely on future preparation, emphasizing learning an array of facts and skills to be used if needed down the road. Active engagement today doesn't preclude a successful future. Rather, it may be the best route toward its realization. The basis for my claim here is that by focusing on building understanding and action competence, we can develop a suite of character skills that equip students for successful engagement in the world today while also providing the disposition and the foundation for long-term, self-directed growth and development.

So what is character? More than just personal honor and integrity, character defines how we approach problems and opportunities, and how we take our place within society. If we accept Dewey's premise about the value of education for today and the future, these are the right issues for kids to be working on, and for teachers to be nurturing. Just what is involved here? David Shields's (2011) framing of four dimensions of personal character and a parallel construct of the overarching community character provides a useful framework for our analysis:

Personal character reflects how we value ourselves and each other, and how we interact with those around us. What is our footprint on the environmental and social landscape? How do we treat others, especially those who are different from or less fortunate than we are?

Civic character describes how we take our place in the larger society. Do we simply make use of what is available to us, or do we also seek to be a contributing member of our community at whatever scale is appropriate for our capacities?

Performance character reflects how we go about the tasks we take on (or for that matter, which tasks we take on). Do we pursue ambitious challenges? Do we have the perseverance to stick with projects and problems—even if they are difficult—until we reach a satisfactory resolution?

Intellectual character describes how we think about issues. Concern here focuses on framing issues fairly, considering multiple points of view, and weighing evidence for its probative value and not simply cherry-picking arguments and evidence to support our preferred cause.

Paired with these individual traits, Shields (2011) offers community character as a meta-level description of the norms guiding the larger community. Does the community value selflessness or self-interest? Long-term or short-term thinking? Local advantage, or regional and global concern? From an educational point of view, community character goes a long way toward defining classroom and school-wide ethics, with a collateral effect on the four dimensions of individual character. A school that rewards only high academic achievers likely places an emphasis on grades as the valued outcome rather than promoting a vision of learning as the result of a sustained effort. This undue emphasis on grades as a marker of merit may deter risk taking and persistence, as well as concern for others and the community. Viewed from another angle, a school that focuses on active citizenship as part of its community character will value civic involvement and strong interpersonal relationships as core values. The over-arching issue here is that what a classroom or school community actually focuses on—beyond the verbiage in the ever-present school mission statement—matters since it focuses effort. With an integrated focus on all four dimensions of character, students' total development can be nurtured.

One of the unfortunate stereotypes of progressive approaches to education that go beyond a nearly exclusive focus on academics is the impression that anything goes, and that there is no intellectual depth. Taken to an extreme, there isn't even a basis for respectfully challenging others' opinions and conclusions, since the emphasis is on everyone feeling good about themselves. While there are schools that set themselves up for such a caricature, this need not be the case. As we will see in Laurillard's design models (taken up in Chapter 4), multiple levels of sustained interaction among students and the teacher can lead to improved formulation of ideas, beyond what the teacher or kids thought when the project started. When teachers design for student engagement, the stereotypical image of student-focused schools as vacuous centers of playtime simply need not be true. Done well, academics and character don't have to be locked in a zero-sum game where emphasis on some outcomes is at the expense of others. In the case of a class focused on active citizenship, a comprehensive approach to character development would value equally the development of performance and intellectual dimensions of character, as well as development of personal and civic character. This is ultimately a matter of building capacity and disposition: The best of intentions won't be enough to solve problems. Instead, any hope of addressing real problems needs to be met with resolve in taking on the challenge, finding the real causes, and working iteratively toward a solution. Intellectual excellence and interpersonal care don't have to be mutually exclusive outcomes.

Building Local to Foster a Sense of Place

Complementing a character-based approach to environmental education, the local or "place-based" focus being advocated for provides an excellent context for students' work. While mass media outlets often highlight large-scale environmental challenges such as deforestation and the plight of the polar bears as ice caps melt, these concerns are in many ways remote to students, even if media outlets bring them into our living room. The multiplicity of causes and the interlocked, inaccessible nature of the underlying drivers for global issues make it difficult for students to chart a path of action that would have a noticeable impact. Based on this limited understanding of what can be done, students either misfire—such as a well-intended effort by a student to save elephants by not buying Ivory soap (Sobel, 1996)—or they lead to token actions such as simply making slogan-based posters on behalf of a cause. Again, well intended but not likely to develop students' action competence or academic skills. Local projects that can be pursued at a scale and complexity appropriate for the students offer a much richer place to start.

Running in parallel with this benefit for students, local projects are at a scale that enables teachers' growth as they have a hand in designing and modifying projects to meet students' needs and interests. Moving past the script of the school-provided curriculum, teachers develop their own pedagogic action competence in crafting and sequencing experiences that bring about growth in their students. It's also quite possible that the teachers themselves develop a better sense of place in their community along with the kids. Many times, our efforts in mentoring teachers have helped them be aware of facets of the community that were previously just an abstraction. When parks become learning laboratories and locations for stewardship projects, everyone wins. Bringing education home, place-based approaches to learning that prioritize local issues can be just the right path for nurturing growth for teachers and students alike.

Threading all of the components of this chapter together, working to understand and act on authentic local issues provides opportunities for kids to develop character as they grow personally and come to value others more, build civic commitment, learn to persist in their efforts toward valued ends, and develop intellectual character by framing issues, learning to hear diverse perspectives, and learning to evaluate relevant data. Through development of these elements of character, action competence is also nurtured since students will better understand the issues and their ramifications, and build commitment to act on what they are learning.

Student Inquiry

If you have followed the argument this far, you may be thinking that this is all sounds good, but there is a critical dimension missing: Exactly what is it that the students do to gain these benefits? While the specific tasks will vary with each project, all of them can be captured under a specific understanding of inquiry. Being careful about the language here is important, since any educator with a modicum of experience knows that the term "inquiry" is overused, covering everything from deep scholarship to the most casual musing. In fact, some nominal inquiry programs for schools offer only a light gloss on meaningful education, as they seek to raise the most basic process of raising a question to an art form. While kids asking questions is absolutely a critically important educational function, calling a question an inquiry is a bit of title inflation.

To be clear in this forest of overuses of the term "inquiry," we need to have some definition. I suggest here that John Dewey's approach to inquiry is sufficiently rigorous for investigations and yet still accessible as a process to comparatively young students. As described in his book *Quest for Certainty*, Dewey (1929/1988) was working throughout his career toward an approach to knowledge that went past relying on forms of knowledge that simply exist externally. In other words, he was working toward framing inquiry as an active, personal quest to know and not just defining knowledge as a process of absorbing facts and ideas that have been put forth as received wisdom. This is a critical distinction for schools, where knowledge is all too often passed along to kids as prepackaged food nuggets to be recalled and displayed on request. Rather, for Dewey true inquiry is built on a persistent quest to frame and address problematic situations. Thus, there is a useful alignment between notions of action competence and character.

Over time, Dewey's effort bore fruit, most notably in his later work *Logic: The Theory of Inquiry* (1938b). Here he described inquiry as "the controlled or directed transformation of an indeterminate situation into one that is so determinate in its constituent distinctions and relations as to convert the elements of the original situation into a unified whole" (pp. 104–105). While this definition is somewhat formal, the underlying intent is clear: Inquiry enables a person to take on a messy, ill-defined situation and—by bringing useful tools and techniques to bear on the situation—arrive at some level of clarity and resolution. This outcome is important to observe, since in a Deweyan sense, an inquiry is not completed until the problematic situation has been resolved in the knower's mind. Simply raising a question is not enough to constitute an inquiry.

As for the specifics of conducting inquiry, Dewey articulates a five-step process in which any step can be revisited as needed. As with the move away from pre-packaged knowledge, this definition of inquiry as an iterative, self-referential process is a significant advance over what students normally encounter as a linear-sequential, lock-step "scientific method" that is immortalized on bulletin boards and school lab reports. Rather, for Dewey inquiry involves traversing these steps as needed:

1. Identifying an "indeterminate" or "problematic" situation
2. Institution of a problem: "To see that a situation requires inquiry"
3. "Determination of a problem-solution"—identifying what factors might be involved
4. "Reasoning" connections to other scientific understandings that may be helpful
5. Determining the "operational character of facts-meanings"—in other words, carrying out "experimental observations" that serve an "evidential function" in resolving the situation.

Thus, in its broad contours, Dewey's approach to inquiry runs parallel to other generic ways of knowing in that situations or problems are identified, inquired upon, and resolved at least to a tentative solution. Two critical differences with the school-based "scientific method" are in the iterative looping allowed in inquiry, and in the criteria for success cited previously. Phrased colloquially, if you haven't brought clarity to the problem, you're not done, so if any of the steps need to be reworked, go back to it. It's not enough to go through the assigned steps and summarize the data in a lab report.

Perhaps an even more profound difference is found in the initial framing of the inquiry. For Dewey (and consistent with learning goals espoused in the rest of this chapter), an assigned topic is not sufficient. Rather, the kids need to participate in defining the scope of the inquiry. Depending on where they are on Hart's ladder of participation, they will likely need adult guidance in structuring the investigation and connecting with school and community resources. Still, it doesn't serve the students to have the questions assigned to them. Identifying issues is critical for students' development, both because of the increased ownership associated with self-determination (Deci & Ryan,

2002), and because of the opportunities it offers students to be involved in the full process of knowing. It's not enough to run the courses set for them: Kids need experience charting a knowledge-building course. Thus, there is the need to frame issues, and not just complete tasks. As Dewey scholar James Scott Johnston (2008, p. 17) notes pithily, "Problem finding is prior to problem solving." Later, he elaborates on this, stating, "Genuine problems must be established before active experimentation takes place, and this requires that students, not teachers or textbooks, legitimate what counts as a problem" (p. 35). Dewey of course would raise a reminder about the essential role of the teacher as the one with the most experience in guiding this process, but he would certainly concur with student involvement in focusing the inquiry. The history of his lab school where many of his educational ideas were first developed is one of active collaboration of teachers and students, with a goal of building capacities in students for their active and immediate use as well as for their long-term growth (Tanner, 1997). There is no question that inquiry in the sense described by Dewey is much more challenging to implement when compared to normal school activities. However, it should be clear by now how this approach to knowing is essential for students if they are to be active learners and achieve ambitious learning goals.

Bringing It All Together: Working on the Work

As this chapter comes to a close, it is time to integrate the many strands of student work introduced here. Action competence, character development, place-based education, and a nuanced view of inquiry all serve as underlying elements for a redefined student experience. To truly re-think environmental education (and the larger educational endeavor of which it is a part), nothing less will do. The history of modern schooling is replete with oscillations between student-focused and subject matter–focused programs, which serve only to pit the child against the curriculum (Dewey, 1902/1990). Similarly, other dualisms drive schooling, and our failure to achieve adequate resolution has kept schools from finding a way forward. Instead, each reform works in isolation to move the pendulum among the different polarities, but to little effect. Instead, we end with a series of partial successes memorably captured by Tyack and Cuban (1997) in their description of school reform as "tinkering toward Utopia."

To create new ground for educational experiences, we need to chart a course that integrates the legitimate values embedded in the different polarities. The child's intellectual growth is important, but so is her ability to become a functioning member of society. To that end, engagement with the important concerns of the larger society needs to be a factor in scoping out educational experiences. Likewise the dualisms between thinking and doing, and process and skill need to be moved past. We need to find ways to simulta-neously nurture character, competence, and sense of place. If we can't do this, school reform will remain on a shuttle train lurching from station to station based on the whims of the moment.

As a path forward, building toward quality work that focuses on actions more than activities is a good place to start. As you will recall, the key differ-ence is that an action has a consequential intention and impact, whereas an activity may be done just for variety or for busywork. At best, an activity can be a contributing part of the process encapsulated in an action as it is described here. Phrased in less academic terms, any teacher or student who hasn't been completely co-opted into the schooling game knows the difference between real work and a school exercise. Recall from the last chapter 11-year-old Ross's shrewd contrast between school and real work when he observed that at school "when it's done it's done and that's your grade." Sidorkin (2010, p. 91) offered a particularly vivid framing of this in characterizing most schoolwork as part of the "wastebasket economy." As he notes, most of what kids do is simply for a grade: "In all cases, despite differences in subject matter, the goal is learning content for purposes of assessment, the chief identity available is that of a stu-dent, and the work primarily involves producing things that eventually end up in a wastebasket."

This despairing note is, unfortunately, all too accurate. Most schoolwork is done in a passive student mode and—if it survives the trip home—is displayed on the refrigerator briefly, tucked in a box, or, most likely, recycled. Once kids are old enough to carry a backpack to and from school, that becomes the final resting spot for students' efforts at least until a parent starts to excavate. As a former teacher I know this denouement all too well, but was recently re-minded of it when I went looking for an example of a traditional math as-signment to use as an illustration for a talk on math education that I was planning. Despite asking a half dozen parents just a few days after the school year had let out, not one had a math paper available. One kind parent went the extra mile and offered to have his daughter "knock off a new one" if I really needed a completed worksheet as a visual for my talk. After all, as he said, "It would only take a minute." Another parent friend has expressed frus-tration that her mathematically brilliant son completes his daily math home-work the morning it is due while he is at the bus stop. Apparently he can do it standing up in just a few minutes. Clearly, we need to "work on the work" if we are to have more meaningful learning experiences.

So, to create work based on action more than activity we need to anchor students' efforts in purposes. This embeddedness gives work it its meaning, as students build valued products. Rheingold and Seaman (2013, p. 4), harken-ing back to Sidorkin, argue that "the value of student work—literally what they make of their labor—at any school depends on many factors including what students produce, why it was created, and who 'uses' or 'consumes' it." Fortunately, there are examples of more successful means of engaging students in real work that we can use as models. For example, King Middle School in Portland, Maine, adopted an Outward Bound / Expeditionary Learning model 20 years ago, using it to frame the core fabric of teacher and student work, and the school's integration with the community. Rather than the traditional model of doing school work and going on an occasional field trip:

> [the] animating discourse at King is for students to approximate the work of professionals, for students to experience application of their work outside of the school, and to shift learning outcomes to align with what people do in the 'real world,' rather than just developing abstract skills and knowledge as they produce things bound for the wastebasket. (Rheingold & Seaman, 2013, pp. 4–5)

This premise of taking on "the work of professionals"—even if only in a metaphorical sense—can serve to drive experiences toward worthy goals. Stepping out of educational contexts for the moment, it is difficult to think of situations in which a person in a real working context is hung up in the dualisms that vex schooling. Whether you are functioning professionally or as an engaged hobbyist, you don't spend time solely in process mode or solely with content. Nor do you just "do" rather than "think." Reframing students' work around valued purposes leads to inherently integrated, non-dualistic experiences.

As a guide, there are a number of strands in the educational literature that converge on this premise. As noted earlier, the framing of action competence presumes a level of authentic engagement with community issues and concerns. Without this, the work doesn't rise to the level of an action, and thus is constrained in its significance. A skeptic might agree with this argument to the extent that such community-based projects are possible, but of course not every component of a sound curriculum lends itself to students taking direct action. Some issues are at too great a distance, or the problem might be occurring at a scale that precludes meaningful direct action. No matter how committed they are, a class of students will not repair the hypoxic "dead zone" in the Gulf of Mexico. Still, is there meaningful work to be undertaken here? This was a challenge undertaken by a high school teacher I have worked with for several years. Being based in St. Louis, Missouri, for us oceans are normally a distant concept. Still, it would be shortsighted for students to graduate from high school without a reasonable engagement with the oceans that cover 70% of the Earth's surface. If we don't want students to work simply for a grade, the solution is to find the link that will bring meaning to their work.

The brilliant solution this teacher developed was to leverage the natural connection. As a river community, we are connected hydrologically to the Gulf of Mexico, and from there to the larger ocean network. As an agricultural state, Missouri is also a large contributor to the fertilizer pollution and sedimentation-causing problems in the Gulf. To add a personal element, these students were generally from upper-middle-class and affluent families that tend to care for their yards intensively. In this way, the teacher was able to forge meaningful connections between an abstract and distant environmental problem spot and the students' home region. Aside from textbook and online research, students learned monitoring techniques to measure key indicators such as nitrates and phosphates through fieldwork with us at the Litzsinger Road Ecology Center. Over the course of their investigations, aspects of the local space—ranging in scale from use of fertilizers on the students' yards to agriculture as one of the dominant industries in the region—connected students with the hypoxic zone more than 600 miles away. This link made ocean processes and ecosystems real to the students, helping them to understand at a very personal level how our choices impact water pollution. As a result, the connection of local streams to their global impact led to informed advocacy within the school community. Clearly this was a sophisticated and ambitious project led by a teacher with higher-than-average agency. She was able to marshal community resources, arrange for this work internally within her school, and craft a pedagogic vision founded on meaningful work for her students.

Another opportunity to build meaningful work arises with complex computer-based simulations. While the default answer within the environmental education world is that students spend too much time inside and are too attached to electronic media, we need to be cautious about introducing a new dualism into our thinking. Simply banishing electronic resources in an effort to "be green" or to ensure "first-hand experience" is overly simplistic and ultimately self-defeating. The key for any resource, whether it be field observations, reference sources like field guides, data collection tools, or simulations, is to consider in which specific ways a given resource adds to the quality of the students' work, which in turn largely determines the educative value of the experience. In this regard, David Williamson Shaffer (Shaffer & Gee, 2006) has established a long-standing research effort into the benefit of what he calls "epistemic games." Well beyond simplistic "be a professional" stereotypes, in an epistemic game successful resolution of the animating challenge requires the player to take on the work role of a professional, whether that be a journalist, lawyer, or engineer. In a similar project drawing on professional norms, the TimeLab 2100 game developed at MIT challenges you to take on the role of a researcher from the future visiting today who is charged with investigating on a handheld device a series of simulated changes in the Cambridge landscape that have occurred due to climate change. Beyond simple information collection and recall, players need to integrate scientific observations and data as they discuss recommendations with their peers about changes that can be made today, in the real world, to mitigate future climate change impacts.

While the Timelab 2100 simulation targets older students, even pre-teen kids can benefit from a locally based epistemic simulation that creates a meaningful work environment. Deanna English, a colleague of mine at the Litzsinger Road Ecology Center, developed a simple but engaging augmented reality game that uses the GPS technology embedded in a smartphone to guide a player around the grounds of the center. As they do this, players "meet" specific parts of the woodland ecosystem, including Stuart Soil, Bella Beetle, Harriet Hawk, and others. When each meeting takes place, the simulated character at that location makes a case for why he or she is the most important part of the ecosystem. Bella Beetle's contributions to decomposition and Susie Squirrel's dispersal efforts need to be considered as students try to address the overarching question of who is the most important part of the forest ecosystem. By the end of the experience, students are equipped to talk with classmates in the role of an ecologist to decide which character is the most important part of the ecosystem. While the original intent was for the students to have a productive experience around concepts of interdependence, a fifth grader correctly pointed out that one of our candidates, Stuart Soil, was actually the most important since he had no plausible replacement. While each of the other functional roles could be replaced with a roughly similar counterpart (e.g., Ollie Oak could stand in for many of the tree functions that Clarence Cottonwood represented), there is no easy substitute for the role of soil within a woodland ecosystem. The larger reminder this provides for us is that when presented with a meaningful and engaging learning environment, students are capable of intellectual work well past that generated for the wastebasket economy.

A key point to keep in mind here is that through a well-designed simulation, students can be engaged in meaningful work that promotes reflective experience on locally relevant issues. When this mediated experience motivates interest in direct action, the benefits multiply. For example, an after-school group of third, fourth, and fifth graders at a nearby school took a winter break from their work restoring a nature trail behind the school. They spent part of that time designing and playing pollinator simulations that modeled the impact of declining bee populations on native plants. The iterative and collaborative nature of the design work fostered the development of personal, performance, and intellectual character as discussed earlier in the chapter. To the extent that it may have sustained interest in the trail project and the larger ecological impact it would have on the community, it might also have served to advance students' civic character. This latter issue—the extent to which games and simulations can motivate interest in real-world action—is an open and interesting research issue colleagues and I are working on.

What Do Teachers Need to Do?

This chapter has sketched a path of intensive involvement for students. By pursuing age-appropriate projects in the local community that they have helped to select and design, even young students can build action competence. Collateral benefits in terms of character development and nurturing a spirit of inquiry speak highly on behalf of this approach to education. Yet despite these benefits, it only happens in selected classrooms. Within the same school, some students have these rich experiences, while others have a more traditional school environment in which students go through the lessons and activities without building toward dynamic and engaging outcomes. This is the conundrum at the heart of the book.

To make sense of it, we need to think carefully about teacher practice. The teachers we find to be more successful in building rich local engagement are animated by a vision of student learning that goes considerably beyond "the wastebasket economy" in which the work is undertaken by mandate, with a primary goal of being assessed for a grade. These high-agency teachers also have the ability to build iteratively and constructively on previous experience. In short, effective teaching in this model is animated by a compelling pedagogic vision and supported by a rich bed of experience. These teachers are also unusually able to marshal resources within their school and the local community, clearing obstacles and calling on "more able assistance" from the community. This process will be sketched out in much more detail in the next chapter.

Bringing that framework to bear on interpreting the student experiences described in this chapter, it should be clear how the teacher's work enables such high-quality learning. For example, think for a moment about the effort linking high school students' Midwestern community to the ocean hundreds of miles away. It's not too hard to imagine what a pro forma ocean unit would look like, with textbook coverage with a lot of text and diagrams, perhaps a video or two, and a lab activity on water salinity. Instead, through her creative vision, their teacher was able to forge a link that made oceans relevant to her students and gave them space to conduct local investigations of water quality that helped to illuminate the scientific basis for the "dead zone." By doing this, the teacher transformed an otherwise standard-issue Earth science unit into an opportunity for her students to sense their connection to the larger world, and more important, to build that connection through constructive action.

Similarly, a dedicated elementary grade teacher in an inner-ring suburb of St. Louis led an after-school group that was focused at the time on local food deserts. Given the diverse community he teaches in, he has students from fairly affluent families as well as students considerably lower on the socio-economic scale. Some families shop at Whole Foods, the upscale natural foods supermarket chain, while others rely on convenience stores since there is no supermarket of any sort nearby. This disparity in access to groceries became clear as students recorded data on their own food practices, mapped data in a geographic information system (GIS) on where food stores were located in the community, and in both cases saw the striking disparities. This work built real understanding. The students took symbolic action by growing their own foods, sparking good discussion of which foods were more nutritious, and the choices people make in their diets. This portion of the larger project helped students come to understand the limits of the food options available in convenience stores. Complementing this work, students benefited from an opportunity to interview a community expert on foods and from my assistance with the use of the GIS tools. As with other projects highlighted throughout the book, the teacher served as the architect, working in collaboration with the students to guide the project's design and implementation.

In these and many other cases, the active agency of the teacher is the key variable in creating a positive and productive learning experience. Once the teacher opens the metaphorical gate, this enables the students to pursue more sophisticated inquiries about their community. Without this, students tend to fall into passive mode within school and, as noted at the outset, all too often pursue more intellectually deep and socially meaningful projects outside of school than they do during the school day. In an effort to further explore this dynamic, the balance of the book analyzes the underlying frames that serve to define teachers' professional roles. Our focus will be on seeing how the ways that teachers frame and go about their work influence the opportunities students have. As we will see, the choices teachers make are animated in part by their frames of childhood. The capabilities and capacity we as educators ascribe to kids make certain choices more or less appropriate. This point is vitally important, since teaching in the United States and in many other cultures takes place against the background of competing paradigms of childhood. As we will see, there is a gaping chasm at work between a largely progressive view of childhood that sees students as sense-makers and capable actors within the community, and an alternative view that focuses on enforced compliance for teachers and kids, and on students' receipt of knowledge and skills to be available for use as needed. How a teacher sees childhood—what kids should do and what they are capable of—goes a long way in terms of framing the work students take on in school. That is the work we turn to next.

CHAPTER 3

Place-Based Education—
Teaching Beyond the Script

I n the two previous chapters, we looked at place-based education as a compelling and engaging way to frame students' work, both in and out of school. By combining intellectually challenging work with opportunities for students to apply the knowledge and skills they are developing, it would appear to be a model for educational reform that is worth emulating. As a further advantage, the opportunity for students to take ownership of their learning can enhance motivation, and thus counter the all too pervasive apathy found in many schools. Despite its potential, however, place-based education struggles to gain traction in a crowded field of competing and contradictory efforts to improve schools. In this chapter and the next, we'll try to gain a better handle on the ways in which the same values that make place-based approaches to learning so compelling also serve to limit its potential for widespread implementation. If a place-based approach to education is to become more widely embraced, we need to better understand the operational and cultural challenges it poses so that implementation efforts can be better positioned for success.

Looking broadly at school reform, for the past half century or more, schools in the United States, Great Britain, and elsewhere have tried to "fix" the educational system in myriad ways, with reform swinging from greater to lesser degrees of control and back again. Recent reform efforts in a number of countries have tried to instill accountability through measures such as increased use of standardized and centralized testing, uniformity in curriculum design (enforced through mandatory adherence to pacing charts), and improved accountability for students' "time on task" by limiting recess and field trips. I've worked with teachers who are held accountable for their class being exactly where they were supposed to be in the detailed lesson plans they filed with the principal, and with (as noted earlier) teachers who need to document even the smallest variation in their plans as real life emerges in the classroom. In the last school I taught in, the administration was quite energetic in touting the benefits of a tracking system that could tell when a child missed a test question whether or not he was in school the day that concept was taught. As a system, it was analogous to each lesson having a postal tracking number attached to its delivery, and once delivered, responsibility for that lesson's use transfers to the recipient (in this case, a child). While the people creating these reforms and enforcing the regulations likely have well-meaning intentions aimed at increasing the quality and scope of learning time, they miss the point. Scripting the delivery of discrete educational fact nuggets and drilling for mastery of procedures that are devoid of context creates a robotic approach to schooling, well distanced from what we know about how people learn and how they find meaning in their lives. Practically speaking, squeezing out every last minute of the school day on tasks of marginal interest and uncertain usefulness serves only to disengage both teachers and students. Increasing time on un-engaging tasks is analogous to a business losing money on every sale but making it up on volume. Ultimately, multiplying negative value is a downward spiral. Designing specifically to achieve this goal is absurd. A key difference, though, is that a corporation with a poorly designed plan either changes or goes out of business. Schools have a way of lingering on, with all but the worst schools taking in a fresh supply of students well past the point at which any "educational freshness date" has been passed.

A key element in preserving space for rich learning experiences is to maintain focus on the critical variable of the teacher. While there are many factors outside the control of the school that affect learning, once a kid gets to school, the biggest factor in his or her success is the teacher's ability to engage kids in meaningful learning. All of the other factors are window dressing around this core premise. Bond issues to fund new facilities and buy new materials may help, but they are secondary to the essential function of a pedagogically dynamic teacher in creating a high-quality learning space. At the other end of the educational spectrum, a student being assigned to a weak teacher has effects documented to linger for years (Borman & Kimball, 2004). A learning environment that is enhanced by ample and useful resources is optimal, of course, but if a choice has to be made, there is no question that a good teacher with mediocre resources will create a better learning environment than a mediocre teacher with even the best resources. In the pages ahead, we'll look at the distinctive qualities exhibited by teachers who create strong, community-engaged learning experiences.

A corollary to the premise of the teacher being the central factor is that despite numerous efforts to revise curriculum plans and supplement them with the latest technology, you can't just buy and install good teaching. Publishers often try to get around this rather inconvenient truth by making teacher-proof curriculum; district administrators create pacing charts to ensure that there is uniform "coverage" and "time on task" in all classes across the district; school boards and politicians measure teacher quality by how well each teacher and school raises student test scores, as if these scores were the best measures of learning or of teacher effectiveness. Each of these efforts builds an external "surround" to bypass the core issues: The teacher has to be equipped to be the primary architect of the students' learning environment, and the teacher must personally embrace and embody the values underlying the curriculum. They need to model curiosity, excitement, and intrigue. Research (e.g., Gresalfi, Barnes, & Cross, 2012) has shown that simply providing a new curriculum is not enough to alter underlying teaching practices. The teacher's values and goals still come through to the students. In turn, this stance has a real impact on how students go about their work. Simply creating and distributing a new script—even if it has been "proved" to work elsewhere—doesn't change how teachers engage their kids. The teacher leading the class has to be in a position to know and decide with personal conviction and enthusiasm that it will work here, for these kids. As Dewey (1938a/1963) remarked 75 years ago:

> Responsibility for selecting the objective conditions carries with it, then, the responsibility for understanding the needs and capacities of the individuals who are learning at a given time. It is not enough that certain materials and methods have proved effective with other individuals at other times. There must be a reason for thinking that they will function in generating an experience that has educative quality with particular individuals at a particular time. (pp. 45–46)

Clearly, Dewey would have trouble with today's highly scripted instruction. Despite the ostensibly good intentions, there are fundamental problems with this level of educational micro-management. A good teacher will rightly feel constrained by prescriptive standardization measures and give up her best practices, find a way to subvert the rules, or simply quit. None of these is a good outcome. It's tragic to see good teachers leave the profession in frustration (or worse, burn out but stay in the classroom!). Equally damning, it's a sign of institutional pathology when the best and brightest practitioners need to engage in subterfuge to serve their students. On the other end of the spectrum, when teachers either start out weak in their practice or become so through discouragement, it can become a lasting problem affecting years' worth of classes. Whatever the cause that led to that point, an un-engaged teacher won't suddenly create a dynamic learning environment just because she is provided a script, a new curriculum, or a mandate requiring her to hit certain coverage benchmarks. Good teaching is an inspired act, not a regulatory process. Over the past quarter century I have worked with a wide range of teachers from the gifted to the . . . less gifted, shall we say. In all that time, I have yet to see a teacher who used to be ineffective suddenly catch fire simply because he was required to. Sadly, many simply drift toward retirement, wasting students' potential learning opportunities along the way.

While issues related to teachers' career development and renewal extend beyond the scope of this book, we need to analyze the spectrum of teaching identities and approaches as we consider how students can best engage with their community, and how teachers can support this process. Before we are done, we'll have a much better handle on why it is often hard for advocates of place-based education to get much "traction" in their efforts to build interest in the practice. As an open question in this regard, I often wonder whether getting place-based education into schools really isn't the problem that needs solving. Rather, the difficulties advocates encounter are a direct outgrowth of a system that—by design—works against the key premises of place-based education, including teacher autonomy, shared decision making with students, and purposeful movement throughout the school and the community. While there are several complex and messy issues that we'll be encountering in the pages ahead, what I am confident of is that we need another, less scripted path to promote inspired teaching and learning. If these more supportive conditions were to be realized, the prospects for place-based education would be greatly improved. From there, it is those activated, highly agentic teachers working in the new paradigm who will be able to determine whether a place-based approach to education is the right strategy for reaching particular goals. This is all that a reasonable advocate of any educational improvement can ask for.

In this chapter and the next we will explore the terrain of professional autonomy and identity specifically as it applies to the design and leadership of place-based education programs. We'll look at how some teachers are able to make effective use of their local environment to support active student investigation and involvement, and how this approach to teaching grows out of significant differences in how they see their work when compared with more traditional approaches to teaching. An argument following directly on this teacher-focused analysis will then be made in Chapter 4: Namely, students who are fortunate enough to be part of such a dynamic environment take on qualitatively different attributes as learners. Most notably, passivity is replaced with an active spirit of investigation that spurs greater interest and commitment. For teachers and students, a virtuous cycle can then begin wherein great teaching motivates learners, whose active engagement in the classroom and the community feeds back into their teachers' enthusiasm and capacity. Logically, the leadership for starting this process has to start with the teachers who inspire engagement in their students. Building from there, nurturing this synergistic loop between teachers and students should be a primary function of everyone in the school. As we will see, administrators play a critical role in enabling this to take place, but the best chance for this to happen is if they themselves are empowered to function as the principal educators (or head teachers) in the school and not just the data monitors and compliance officers. While the discussion here focuses on the role of teachers' agency in overcoming scripted constraints, there is an equally important discussion to have about how many talented administrators find themselves just as scripted in their scope of responsibility.

Before we get into the crux of the issues, a context note: It's true that the model to be presented here describing the pedagogic agency displayed by place-based teachers can be extrapolated to other curriculum approaches and innovations that rely on active teaching. In the interests of keeping the book to a manageable size for the author and the reader, the broader issues will be left to another time. For now, place-based education provides a good focal point for thinking about the larger and very important goal of teaching beyond the script since it is here that teachers really "show their stuff." With few if any packaged, locally based curriculum materials available, the entire project bypasses the possibility of a slick teacher-proof curriculum acting as a crutch for active decision making. Instead, projects are locally built through innovation and commitment. Also, since these local projects rarely enter directly into the district- and state-approved curriculum, teachers often need to develop strategies for addressing formal coverage requirements in creative ways. For example, math requirements are commonly met through local data collection efforts, while language arts skills are developed through local journalism projects and blogs describing students' stewardship efforts.

With a little creativity, even whole units of required curriculum can be re-centered into the community and aligned for better learning. One school I worked with for a few years thought their field studies with us ended with their fifth grade ecology unit since there was no life science in sixth grade (the capstone year at that school). With a bit of consultation from me, the teacher got creative and shifted the focus of her mandated chemistry unit to a base in water-quality monitoring. This refocusing of the unit enabled the students to spend the fall of their sixth grade year investigating water chemistry, with an emphasis on how good water chemistry supports healthy aquatic life. The kids still covered key concepts like acids, bases, chemical mixtures, and lab procedures, but did so with a renewed purpose not found in previous years. Tests conducted on creek and pond water samples served to give them a solid lab experience to complement their fieldwork, and the data sets they generated built science process and math skills. Through this curricular restitching, students integrated their new awareness of creek insects, water quality, and the like into an expanded understanding of the local ecosystems they had just studied the previous spring. Thus, with just a little creativity, greater linkages were made to create continuity between formerly discrete science units, which in turn created greater synergy between the formal learning requirements and students' connection to local ecosystems. One more unit moved out from the classroom to the community, and one more teacher took ownership of the curriculum sequence she was handed.

As examples like this will show throughout the book, committed place-based teachers are able to create something special for their students. Working around the edges, either in partnership with the administration or at least with their tacit approval, these teachers routinely go beyond scripted instruction. The model of agency to be offered here provides a description of how teachers can do this, and in the process reclaim the professional identity that has eroded over the past decade or more of standardization. It all comes down to the teacher's ability and willingness to assert control of his or her practice by making judicious decisions that are based in a deeply held, carefully cultivated educational vision and set of values.

Decisions, Decisions: Making Educational Values Come to Life

In most cases, the act of making a decision implies both a set of intended outcomes, and an assumed capacity for these intentions to be realized, either directly by the person making the decision or by people who will be influenced by the decision. Without an intention and potential for its realization, the act of making a decision would likely be a futile exercise. Moved from a general consideration of decision making to a specifically educational context, the intended outcomes are usually framed jointly by the teacher's overarching vision of successful learning, and by any specific curriculum expectations for which the teacher is held responsible. Bound up within the issue of a capacity for these intentions to be realized are considerations of the teacher's own personal and professional capacities, the students' capacities, and an assortment of institutional capacities (such as space, equipment, and collegial support).

Taken together, the complex range of intended outcomes and the factors affecting capacity can make what seems to be a fairly simple decision into a quite complicated process. When we stop to truss up a decision for analysis, this complexity becomes self-evident. The classic teacher question of "What do we do on Monday?" can in fact be a pretty deep question if the teacher is acting with some level of pedagogic agency. Moving off-script into what amounts to a well-founded improvisational act opens many possibilities that need to be considered and acted on, often on the spur of the moment. When a teacher needs to redirect Johnny's behavior, she doesn't have time for a consultation with the school psychologist, time to attend a workshop, or time to conduct a literature review on proven strategies. She needs to act now, based on her reading of the situation, her instincts, and her values.

Despite the complexity of most classroom situations, in practice teachers make most of their decisions quickly and seemingly effortlessly. What is it that guides the paths taken and those not taken? As we will see, differences among teachers in how they frame their jobs, their understanding of the general nature of learning, and their vision of students' capacities lead to a wide divergence in the decisions they arrive at. In terms of impact, the many great and small decisions teachers arrive at cluster together to define the learning environment that their students experience. In assessing the effectiveness of the teacher's decisions specifically in terms of how they promote or inhibit place-based inquiry, we need to remember the broader principle that intentions only make sense in light of the culture or set of values within which the action takes place. Values animate the rest of the decision-making process, so it is here that we begin.

When looking at values, it's important to remember that what makes sense in realizing one set of values may not be reasonable or appropriate in another. Goffman (1986) cites a historical example of a Native American being sent to Harvard to be "educated," but his tribe couldn't see the value in this since what was learned had no value in their Native culture. What in Western culture is seen by many as the pinnacle of education was seen by the Native Americans as largely worthless. Here, we're looking for ways to build a learning culture that supports the development of certain attributes among students, including initiative, independent thought, and the ability to sustain interest in an inquiry through to its completion. Thus, our work is laden with certain values, informed by a belief that place-based approaches to education and the underlying values of teacher and student ownership of the learning process are worth advocating for. Bateson's (2000) conception of frames as "a spatial and temporal bounding of a set of interactive messages" (p. 191) is helpful here. He argues that frames help both to *include* and to *exclude*, drawing attention to certain ideas or experiences that make sense relative to each other. Practically speaking, Bateson suggests that it isn't helpful to use the same thinking *outside* of the frame that you would *inside* the frame. A parallel argument from the world of games is made through the concept of the magic circle (Huizinga, 1971), where players willingly take on rules inside the game that make no sense outside of the game. For example, there are many more efficient ways to get a golf ball in the hole than using a series of clubs at a distance, but that's an accepted part of the game. Within the magic circle of golf, use of the club is the only acceptable option. Similarly, for a place-based teacher, designing for certain values such as student initiative, independent thought, and commitment to sustained inquiry is the only way to play school.

Looking more broadly at educational values, what makes sense in one teaching frame is odd, irrelevant, or inappropriate in another. Early in my career I was teaching in a large suburban elementary school. As a recent graduate of a very progressive teacher preparation program, I tried to make the classroom space as open and accessible to the students as possible. Before long, the kids claimed the closet as a preferred work space, to the point that we had to work out a rotation of which students were allowed to work there each day and a set of rules for its use. I learned later in the year that one of the other teachers in the school was the subject of complaints from parents to the administrators since students in her class were sent to work in the closet for discipline. Note that in both cases, the act in question was the same—fifth graders working in the closet—but that the values attached to the pedagogic decisions were quite different. My colleague and I were operating from different value frames, and in turn others judged our actions based on their own values. I was considered too lax by some for allowing students that much freedom, while my colleague was seen as too strict and repressive for requiring exactly the same act that my students sought after on their own. Framed within different sets of educational values, each perspective had some validity. From the students' perspective, many saw the closet as a clubhouse of sorts within an impersonal 1,200-student elementary school, while others were sent to it as a place of shame, again, framing matters since it calls into play our deepest educational values.

Specific to our focus here on better understanding the challenges and opportunities offered by place-based education, we need to pay particular attention to the "culture gap" between compliance-driven, highly scripted approaches to learning and more active student-focused, community-based approaches. Given this difference in approaches, passing judgment on the appropriateness of educational decisions can only be done in reference to the underlying goals and values. Thus, we need to be clear about which values are meant to prevail. An administrator whose teaching framework puts a high value on adherence to the prescribed curriculum will likely see a very structured and tightly scheduled class and think, "That's a really great teacher. Her kids are lucky to have her." Conversely, a second administrator focused on students as co-creators of learning environments will likely see such a regimented classroom environment as overly structured, and thus depriving students of chances to take ownership of their learning. On the one hand the teacher models a traditionally defined sense of order; on the other had, there is very real potential for passivity and apathy growing among the students. Given a chance to intervene, the first administrator would attempt to maintain the status quo and hold it up as an exemplar, while the other would likely encourage a series of paradigm shifts to reframe classroom norms toward shared ownership between the teacher and her students.

As these examples show, in many ways it's how you see an act that gives it legitimacy. Unless taken to an extreme, there is no clearly right or wrong pedagogy, and no amount of data-driven management will result in a "proven practice." Rather, as Shapiro and Biber (1972) remark, "One treads a rough path between knowledge and opinion. Certain facts seem well substantiated, many are open to question, others remain an article of faith" (p. 61). Different personal and professional values bestow (or withhold) legitimacy on a school environment. As a result, we have open schools such as Summerhill (Neill, 1960), as well as highly prescriptive models such as Success for All (Lemann, 1998) that dictate in great detail the curriculum sequences all teachers and students are expected to follow.

Following on the analysis in Chapters 1 and 2 describing the scope and nature of place-based education, it's clear that the underlying framework for success in that frame needs to be largely "progressive" in a Deweyan sense.[1] This approach places a high value on both teachers and students exercising agency as they co-create learning experiences and work together toward making a definable impact on the community in which they live. Echoing Dewey, most place-based educators believe that education should be about students' lives today, not simply focused on preparation for a future life. Consequently, we put less stock in educational programs that are overly future-oriented and that don't provide a meaningful focus on equipping children to gain the most meaning out of life today. This isn't to exclude an eye toward the future, but it does reflect a recognition that the best way to thrive as an 11-year-old is to have a vibrant and fulfilling life as a 10-year-old. Key parameters advanced by Dewey in *Experience and Education* (1938a/1963), including the progressive development of subject matter over time and the importance of connecting students' new experiences to what has gone before, provide essential guidance in navigating this present–future tension.

Looking specifically at the teacher's role in structuring the learning environment, Dewey (1897/1964) argued:

> The teacher is not in the school to impose certain ideas or to form certain habits in the child, but is there as a member of the community to select the influences which shall affect the child and to assist him in properly responding to these influences. (p. 432)

Be sure to catch here the leadership function ascribed to teachers. Giving students ownership does not mean the teacher can abdicate. Instead, the teacher is expected to be the senior member of the group. Unlike completely democratic schools such as Summerhill (Neill, 1960) and the Sudbury Valley School (Greenberg, 1995) where teachers and students have an equal voice, education in a Deweyan sense assumes adult leadership. Not having this, Dewey (1938a/1963) argues, devalues the greater life experience of the teacher. As we will see later in the chapter, this "progressive-style" framing of

---

[1] It's important when we use the term "progressive" to remember that Dewey himself expressed great concern in *Experience and Education* (1938a/1963) about what he saw as loose and ill-conceived ways in which his ideas were being used under the progressive banner.

the teacher's role as the leader in a co-construction environment is essential for meaningful student engagement with the community.

Who Makes the Decisions, and How?

The crux of effective teaching starts with the pedagogic decisions teachers make. As the previous discussion of values makes clear, there are no neutral decisions. They all embed values, implicitly or explicitly. This is true both at the meta-level where decisions are made about the overarching goals of a given project and its intended learning outcomes, and at the micro-level, considering the many interactions teachers have with students as the work unfolds. Over the past decade, the move toward rigid curriculum sequences has given great privilege to a set of educational values that has all but removed meaningful decision making from the realm of the teacher. Instead, current policies favor a standardization that is designed and managed by distant administrators and disembodied policy documents. When every minute of the day needs to be pre-approved in a lesson plan, professional discretion is being severely compromised. We should also make a side note just to call attention to the elephant in the room: In the United States and other places that favor centralized educational planning, district and state assessment tools also serve to shape the work, as the values and measures guiding the assessment of teacher and student performance tend to play an outsized role in determining what happens in the classroom.

Left to drive the curriculum, the standardization mindset that dominates current educational thinking today favors tightly efficient delivery over nuanced professional judgment. Consequently, we end up with curriculum that is designed for efficient delivery over pedagogic effectiveness, such as an ecology unit focused on seasonal change being scheduled for a six-week curriculum slot rather than being structured to capture dynamic changes in the landscape over the course of the full school year. The most extreme case of this delivery mindset I've encountered was a plan whereby a local district sequenced their elementary grade science units in a pair of three-year cycles (kindergarten through second grade, and then third through fifth grade). Under this plan all of the students in third through fifth grades would be studying the same plant unit at the same time across the district. The point at which a particular science concept was introduced became a function of the year of the child's birth, as did the sequential order of the units. This approach definitely created an efficiency in terms of being able to provide district-wide professional development for teachers (who in fact did need a lot of help in implementing a functional science program), but at what cost to the coherence of the teachers' or the students' experiences? Aside from the lack of continuity in the kids' science programs, the net effect on teachers was that they would encounter a unit only every three years under this plan, which works against their ability to develop competence and confidence in teaching that unit. In practice, this strategy reinforces the problem it was meant to solve relating to teacher capacity. It creates a dependence on quick in-service workshops to gain tips and tricks for completing the new units, rather than fostering a level of pedagogic content expertise that is needed for excellent teaching but that can only be developed over time.

Along with this removal of curricular decision-making authority in favor of a delivery mindset, we also need to acknowledge the extent to which data-informed decision making is currently all the rage. The underlying assumption here is that a table of assessment data makes it obvious what needs to be done to remedy student deficits. For example, the typical response to a student who has low scores on a test of "math facts" is that clearly he needs remediation drills until his scores improve. After all, poor math skills will keep him from enjoying a career in one of the highly desired and prestigious STEM fields (science, technology, engineering, mathematics), and the nation will be less competitive as a result. Or so traditional logic dictates. Before the syllogism train completely leaves the station, we should put the brakes on and look at alternative ways of seeing the situation. There are a number of possibilities to explore. Perhaps the student in question has a weak understanding of an underlying concept such as number patterns or place value, which in turn will limit developing a good understanding of times tables. Or, maybe he's a strong math student who just had a bad day when the test was taken. The same test taken tomorrow may have a different result. While educators may be hesitant to admit it, maybe he just hates math class or his teacher and he couldn't care less what his grade is. Viewed in a larger perspective, this whole discussion assumes that the test is a valid measure of a child's mathematical capacity. Research has shown that people who are marginal performers on a computation test can be wizards at determining the most cost-effective purchase at a supermarket or in acting as a street vendor (Lave, 1988; Lockhart, 2009). Data-paradigms aside, it's a simple fact that tested skills don't necessarily correlate with ability or understanding.

Linking back to the micro-management issue, instances in which teachers do have even a modicum of discretion are usually found where test scores are acceptable. This is true both within a building, where teachers often report that "as long as my scores are OK, my principal lets me make choices," and at a district level, where my experience has been that teachers in affluent districts have more discretion over the curriculum than in school districts where test scores are close to the margin of acceptability. The equity issues here should be obvious.

Given the increasing tide of standardized and test-driven teaching, the heroic efforts of the place-based teachers who can break out of this educational

Flatland are all the more noteworthy. Effective teachers know that context is critical when it comes to learning, and that real understanding takes nurturance and time to emerge. Good data are useful, but we need to remember that at most, data indicating low-level performance are a presenting symptom, not a diagnosis. More generally, we need to recognize that not every aspect of professional practice can be reduced to a simple if-then statement and solution. As Donald Schon (1983) notes in regard to effective professional practice in any field, "Situations of practice are not problems to be solved but problematic situations characterized by uncertainty, disorder, and indeterminacy" (pp. 15–16). If we accept Schon's general premise as being valid for schools, we need to look more critically at how educational situations are framed and how decisions are made, and restore this work to the level at which it can do the most good: in the hands of competent teachers who are ready to implement constructive planning on behalf of students.

Unfortunately, as we have seen, this heretical notion has been all but banished in most schools. Salvatore Vascellaro (2011) captures the professional impoverishment of teachers' work spaces as he notes:

> a trend in which teachers are being given scripts, precise vocabulary, and rigid sequences, regardless of who the children are and what their experience has been. Quite literally, the children are bypassed. It is important to realize that the teacher is also bypassed. New teachers tend to need guidance, but does telling them exactly what to do promote their growth as professionals? The learning process is reduced to technique and the teacher reduced to a technician. Perhaps most harmful is how easy it is for teachers to rely on the directions and not see themselves as capable decision makers. (p. 70)

Perhaps most disheartening, the modern characterization of "good" schools as rote learning environments is not substantially different from what it was nearly a century ago. In a study of school culture at the turn of the 20th century, Angelo Patri (1997) noted very similar challenges of innovative and committed teachers encountering bureaucratic resistance and the more general pattern of dominant school cultures favoring conformity over creativity. Today we have simply codified the practice into state and local district policies. Despite more than a century of emerging insight into how people learn, we seem bent on continuing to live out Dickens's parody of "facts" as the basis for schooling as it was memorably captured in his novel *Hard Times*. As Seymour Papert observed at the beginning of his book *The Children's Machine* (1994), fields such as medicine have advanced in their vision, technique, and resources quite a bit over the years, while all but the most exceptional school remains stuck in a paradigm dating back at least into the 1800s. In a shrewd vignette, Papert captures how a doctor from the 1800s would be shocked by today's operating room, while a teacher would find much that is familiar.

Despite this gloomy view of the educational horizon, all is not lost. We have ample evidence that effective teachers are able to venture beyond the official script to make well-informed choices that reflect their understanding of students' needs and interests. By re-jiggering the sequences of curriculum units or fostering greater connections among the nominally discrete units (like the bridge from fifth grade ecology to sixth grade water chemistry described earlier), teachers can create a more holistic experience for their students. This more active stance taken by teachers also typically involves a driving ambition to leverage resources beyond the assigned curriculum materials. Conversely, some of the least engaging and least productive classrooms are the ones in which everyone in the room is going through the motions, following a script not of their own making. Reflexivity—the ability of one experience to feed into the next—is largely absent both for the teacher and the students, as each day is pretty much like the one before and a good preview of what is to come. If anything, entropy seeps in, draining energy from teachers' and students' work. As Susan Rosenholtz (1991) found, there is a wide and persistent gap between teachers who are certain in their pedagogic choices and lead non-routine (read: stimulating and variety-filled) classrooms and those who are less certain and confident of their beliefs and who lead passive, routine classes.

What Does Good Decision Making Look Like?— The Importance of Vision

If we are to restore decision making to teachers, what can we expect their decisions to look like? Most of the really important educational decisions are judgment calls in response to what Schon referred to as "problematic situations." In these cases, the best answer isn't always obvious to an uninformed outside observer, or for that matter to an inexperienced teacher. With a good chunk of my professional work now being devoted to mentoring teachers, I see teachers who work over the course of years to build a repertoire of responses to situations, and more foundationally, build their ability to "read" a class's needs, weigh options, and make decisions. Effective teachers are always asking themselves questions along the lines of *"Out of all of the possible directions we could take, which is the best direction for these kids at this time?"* More than simple problem solving around behavior problems or curriculum coverage, sometimes teachers need to engage in "problem finding" (Sennett, 2008, p. 9), identifying emerging needs as they are exhibited by individual students or by the class as a whole. In response, these more active teachers create new learning experiences on the fly that weren't originally planned. Throughout, making sound decisions requires a level of professional agency that requires the teacher to be equipped to evaluate the situation and make a responsive and responsible choice. That choice in turn is based simultaneously on her vision of what successful learning looks like, and on constructive use of her past experience. Thus, reading the classroom landscape with nuanced judgment is essential, as is awareness of a range of alternative decision paths.

Emirbayer and Mische (1998) offer a framework for agency that we can adapt to help us understand just how this decision making happens. The first premise in their framework is that a teacher's decisions are informed by the vision he or she holds for effective learning. A teacher who values student autonomy and self-guided inquiry will value certain outcomes more than a teacher for whom order and discipline are paramount. Within the same broad topic—say, a watershed study—these different values will lead two different teachers to work toward diverging goals. The teacher focused on student autonomy would likely emphasize exploratory investigations to start, leading toward a project developed jointly by the teacher and students. A teacher focused on having his students gain experience with the canonical scientific method may still engage a class in a watershed study, but he is more likely to value careful advance preparation focused on students' learning the steps involved in his preferred model of the scientific method, developing facility with relevant water-testing protocols, and applying these efforts toward a predefined data collection and reporting effort. Neither of these framings is inherently better than the other. Rather, each emerges out of a set of pedagogic values the teacher has developed over time. Looking across the landscape, each of these two hypothetical teachers may well see the other as not fulfilling her professional mandate. To borrow liberally from the "The Story of the Three Bears," it's easy to see teaching approaches as being too loose or too tight. Or if you prefer, the late comedian George Carlin had a brilliant sketch parodying how when we drive we always fall into the perfect speed. Everyone else who is faster than we are is driving like a maniac, while those who are slower must have something wrong with them. Returning to the classroom context, teachers need to craft a learning space that is "just right" in speed and size for *these* kids at *this* point in time. What they choose depends on their vision of what good learning involves.

This expert judgment in designing environments is of course easier said than done. Looking for the optimal way to structure students' experiences has been a perennial quest for educators. The constant element is that these structuring decisions are informed by a particular vision of successful learning, which in turn draws on an implicit or explicit understanding of what it means to know something and on a particular view of childhood. Phrased very generally, a teacher who sees the child as an autonomous sense-maker will frame decisions differently than would a teacher who is operating from an implicit view of a child as a "sponge" or a blank slate whose job is to assimilate new material with a goal of being able to replicate knowledge on demand. The impact of these competing epistemic visions—or beliefs in how people come to know— that are held by teachers cannot be overstated in terms of their relative value for supporting place-based education. Projects such as the fifth grade native plant garden highlighted earlier require a more active stance toward knowledge and the process of coming to know than is typical for many science classes. Even if we leave aside as inadequate a purely textbook-driven unit on plants, a more typical activity-based botany unit might have kids plant a bean seed and maybe do some controlled comparisons of the impact of different watering levels on plant growth. These simple projects are certainly better than just reading about plants, but there is still a difference here between this work and a more active pursuit of understanding that is embedded in action. In designing and creating the garden, the kids needed to use multiple text and human sources for information. They also needed to understand and balance key variables affecting plant growth such as sunlight, water, and soil type. Finally, they needed to use their emerging understanding as the basis for taking on a publicly visible stewardship responsibility. Viewed as a whole, the vision of learning underlying a place-based project like this is much more ambitious than is usually found in a traditional classroom. This difference in vision presents a challenge and an opportunity.

Reliving the Past

Continuing our analysis of teachers' decision-making processes and how they impact capacity for place-based learning, we have one more dimension to consider. In addition to the nexus of factors that converge on the specific decision(s) to be made, and the epistemic vision that informs those decisions, a third critical dimension comes into play. This is the extent to which a teacher can draw on past experience productively. A somewhat overstated distinction is often made between a teacher with 20 years of experience and a teacher with 1 year of experience repeated 20 times. The first one has engaged in a practice of iterative improvements made in response to each year's successes, challenges, and opportunities, whereas the second one focuses more on compliance with the "teacher script," whether it be an external script assigned from a teacher-proof curriculum or simply an internalized image of what it means to be a teacher. More likely, it is a synthesis of the two. While no one could claim that a person doesn't learn *anything* over time, the truism has a degree of merit in it that is relevant to our concerns here. Active place-based teaching that goes beyond the given curriculum is an adventure, requiring substantial iterative growth over time in local knowledge, practical wisdom, and ability to engage and lead kids. Given this, clearly the instance of 20 increasingly rich years of experience—with the teacher as an active and reflective decision maker—is preferable, both in the kids' interest and in the teacher's own self-interest. Without this iterative growth, both teacher and students risk falling into Mills's (1959/2000, p. 171) "cheerful robot" model. As we have seen, place-based education, and the progressive tradition of education from which it springs, assumes active, responsible thinking and an effort toward substantive growth over time.

Ultimately, as we just noted, teaching decisions need to be well-informed choices that align with a compelling vision for successful learning. If teachers respond on autopilot, abdicate this decision making to the scriptwriters, or are otherwise poorly equipped to make these decisions, the results won't serve the students nearly as well. Life in active classrooms involves too many ad hoc decisions for which answers simply can't be pre-specified. There are better and less good choices, but they remain just that: choices that need to be made in situ. Doing so by drawing from a well-tended bed of experience allows for judgment that is informed by the nuances of the situation. The same epistemic and pedagogic values that help to define our forward-looking vision help to steer efforts to draw on past experience as well, since teachers need to make selective withdrawals from this bank of experience. The choice of which withdrawals to make will inevitably be based on the extent to which the teacher believes that previous efforts can be useful in informing the current decision to be made. On one hand, if you don't value project-based outdoor learning, you will look with little favor on past experiences and perhaps give undue weight to the problems you encountered last time. (There were too many bugs, the kids were wild once we got outside, and so on.) On the other hand, a generally favorable view of outdoor learning might lead the teacher to give more weight to the positive benefits realized last time, and prompt reflections or requests to peers for advice on how to improve the experience. How teachers frame an experience will go a long way in determining what they get out of it, and how willing they are to return to it and rework it toward improvement.

This need for active involvement in all phases of decision making is particularly true in leading rich community-based projects, which as we have noted generally have no script. Deferring to an external authority like a textbook really isn't an option (which might at least partially explain why script-oriented teachers and schools are quite often hesitant to take their kids outside). Instead, all but the most basic community-based projects are improvisation acts pursued individually or with colleagues. Even a project that is repeated year to year requires some modifications to reflect new opportunities or changing circumstances. When place-based education is done well, teachers draw from their past experience with similar projects in a way that informs current decision making. This requires a process of literal *re-vision*, or seeing the past in ways that bring useful information forward. Even if the project didn't meet its goals, it can be fodder for reflection leading to modifications or even a whole new project next time. Instead of responding to a struggling project with a dismissive comment such as "It didn't work last time; . . . let's not do that again," effective place-based teachers have a store of experiences that can be drawn from to inform—but not dictate—their current choices. Recall the advice from Dewey offered earlier suggesting that teachers need to make choices for what will work in *this* case and for *these* kids. It's not sufficient to say that something was proved to work for other kids elsewhere and therefore it must work here. It's also not helpful to say that since something didn't work before, it can't be made to work through considered re-visioning of the experience. Like the handyman with a lot of spare parts on hand, teachers need to be able to access and re-purpose bits of the past to address a current concern.

To summarize the argument to this point, teachers need to make decisions that are based on a vision of success and that are informed by a re-visioning of their past experiences. Both of these aspects of decision making are highly contingent on the teacher's epistemic vision as it encompasses what counts as knowledge and how people learn. This vision in turn draws forth elements that are useful in determining just what the pedagogic issues are, and what the best response might be. In navigating this decision-making process, teachers exhibit what Schon (1983) has called "reflection in action" and "knowing in action," processes that draw on our tacit ability to navigate the "complexity, uncertainty, instability, uniqueness, and value-conflict" inherent in professional practice (p. 39). This is inevitably a complex process that requires more of teachers personally and professionally than reliance on what Schon calls a "technical rationality" (p. 21) based on scripted, data-driven instruction. While schools may have an institutional bias toward this latter approach, the vision of teaching and learning that is essential for place-based education requires much more agency on the part of the teacher, informed by ongoing reflection and knowing in action.

Looking at the Broader Community of Practice

The argument made here about decision making is fine as far as it goes, but it doesn't reflect the full scope of teachers' practice. With liberties taken from John Donne, no teacher functions as an island unto him- or herself. Instead, many people will have input on what should happen at school, since education is ultimately a public trust. Students, parents, colleagues, administrators, and community members all have a legitimate stake in the classroom, and thus are in a position to influence decision making. Ideally, these stakeholders will exercise wise judgment and be in a position to contribute to the quality and scope of the learning environment. The reality, of course, is that these external influences can be positive or negative in terms of support for goals we espouse. As we will see in Chapter 5, many popular understandings of what counts as "good" education are driven by visions of schooling and childhood that work counter to the values embedded in place-based education. Obviously, this poses some real challenges in advocating for more use of community engagement as a teaching framework.

Beyond human influences, it's also important to recognize that resources matter, too. Earlier I made the claim that a strong teacher with mediocre resources would do better than a mediocre teacher with ample resources. Still, even though school budgets all too often deny this reality, resources do make a difference in the quality of students' experiences. Regarding budgets, an experience early in my teaching career in which I was met with puzzled expressions when I asked about a supply budget for my science classes—after all, the school had just bought new textbooks—is sadly all too common. When we have grant-funded programs that support materials for implementation, it's striking how many teachers need to use the grant funds for basics like markers and graph paper just to be able to do simple projects. Beyond these basic supplies, access to interesting resources in the community is important for place-based education to thrive. Great teaching is foundational, but resources—whether they be human, material, or situational in nature—do matter.

In her book *Redesigning Learning Contexts*, Rosemary Luckin (2010) has analyzed the interplay of several of these influences to understand better how what she calls the "ecology of resources" (p. 90) available to a learner supports educational growth. In her framework, this ecology includes both the human and material resources that are available, though increasingly we also need to account for the virtual resources that are available to support learning. One of the most intriguing parts of Luckin's framing is her adaptation of Vygotsky's zone of proximal development into a zone of available assistance (p. 28). This has implications both for the teacher in the use of pedagogic experts to guide the design and implementation of place-based projects, and in the use of community leaders to mentor students in their efforts. We can apply Luckin's ecology of resources framework directly to extend the decision-making model presented in this chapter, as it provides greater clarity in our quest to understand the factors that influence teachers' decision making. By considering the ecology of resources available to a teacher (and the ways in which a teacher leverages these resources), we can gain greater insight into how some learning environments are more robust and productive than others. There are three broad dimensions in Luckin's model to consider here:

First, there is a range of people and tools that can be used productively to support student inquiries. For example, a fourth grade class I worked with recently brought in an expert on local foods from a nearby grocery store to share information that was relevant to the students' investigation of issues related to community food justice. This added information provided "just in time" knowledge and perspectives that students didn't have access to within their school setting and that the teacher struggled to find online in a kid-friendly format. Similarly, a number of teachers in our community seek out the support of horticulture experts on my staff to provide constructive feedback to students on their designs for a native plant garden. For these projects, we usually end up affirming much of what the students propose, but make some specific recommendations to the students when their plant choices might not be optimal given botanical considerations (such as the plants' need for sunlight and water) or pragmatic concerns (how it would look relative to other nearby plants, or how hardy it would be with the inevitable playground foot traffic). The teacher can then work with the students to adjust their plans in response to the expert feedback. The entire consultation process serves to deepen the students' general understanding of botany and ecology, link this understanding to issues specific to Missouri native plants, and create awareness of horticulture as a science-related career.

More generally, any effort to connect students to community experts relies on a good bit of judicious decision making on the part of the teacher, as it requires selecting people based on their relevant expertise and their ability to connect with students at their level of understanding and maturity. While many professionals will not have expertise in working with kids, they do need at least an instinctual ability to connect with young learners in a way that builds understanding. Pedantic lecturers may know a lot, but if that information isn't structured in a way that supports student learning and engagement, the educational benefits will be minimal. Expert conceptual networks can easily become meaningless for younger students who don't have the experience or cognitive sophistication to understand what is being presented. Pretty quickly, the kids shut down mentally and become bored or restless. At best, expert terms that are devoid of understanding will be parroted back on request for a while, but the overall effort will not make a useful contribution to the students' learning. On the other end of the spectrum, someone who is great with the kids but unable to help them develop useful understanding will also have a limited impact on their educational growth. Neither pompous pedantry nor fuzzy feel-good approaches to education serve kids well. A resourceful teacher knows how to navigate between the two poles in selecting outside assistance.

Just as community experts can extend student investigations, a range of tools can be employed productively. For example, we had a middle school in rural Missouri participate in both of the National Science Foundation–supported after-school projects we led (Local Investigations of Natural Science and Community Science Investigators). Over this extended period of collaboration the teachers and their students developed facility with use of the use of geographic information system (GIS) and global positioning system (GPS) tools to support a variety of local investigations involving local streams, ethnic food access, and public awareness of community resources. The students' geospatial skills came in handy when a string of decidedly out-of-season tornados hit in the area in late December. Returning from their winter break energized by the recent natural disaster, students were quickly able to draw on their skills to map current and historical tornado data, which led to an interesting surprise: Despite Missouri being considered part of the United States' "tornado alley," not a single tornado was shown in their county for the 50-year period of record in the data set. Still, the event and its aftermath motivated the students to investigate tornado safety in greater detail, and create and lead an educational program for elementary-age students in the district.

In another application of tools for place-based learning, I worked with a pair of fifth graders from a different school who used Vernier probes, GIS software, and GPS receivers as part of a science fair project designed to map changes in the water quality along a local creek (Coulter, 2000a). By plotting the water-quality data on a map along with related data on local land use and known pollution-discharge sites in the watershed, the fifth graders were able to make sense of water quality issues in the community with some degree of sophistication. As they noted in their analysis, "The water [quality] did differ from site to site along the creek because of the varying environments through which the creek runs . . . . After a careful inspection of our data, we concluded that site three showed the most interesting variation because the water quality at site one is good, site two is good, the site three is bad, and site four is good." This anomaly led to a careful analysis not only of what factors in the watershed would make the third site worse than two of the upstream sites, but also of what might have led to the fourth site still further downstream to have improved conditions.

In both the tornado and the creek projects, the use of relatively advanced tools supported the investigations in ways that simple data collecting and graphing of the resultant data would not have allowed. High-quality teaching and student engagement are foundational to the whole process, but having access to good tools does matter. The key for effective use of tools is in making productive choices concerning which ones have the power to support productive inquiry while not overwhelming students. Not enough power will leave the job undone, or make it very time consuming to complete. Conversely, too powerful and complex a tool will lead to frustration or simply be a waste of time. A GIS is a very powerful analytical tool, but learning it simply to complete one activity is a poor use of instructional time. In both of the cases cited here, GIS was a good choice, as someone whom Luckin (2010) would describe as being able to provide "more able assistance" was able scaffold the use of the software with the kids. This assistance enabled the students to focus on the investigation at hand without getting bogged down in the nuances of professional-grade software.

In making decisions, teachers need to resolve a tool dilemma of sorts: On the one hand, without having access to the right tools, projects like the ones described here would lose much of their analytical depth and consequently their educational value. On the other hand, not having effective scaffolding tools can cause frustration for the students and cut off their learning. Both the value and potential trade-offs have to be considered in making tool choices. As any craftsperson knows, having access to the right equipment and knowing when (and how) to use it matters if you are to get the job done.

Consistent with these examples, Luckin (2010) argues that teachers need to have a good "filter" on the use of both experts and tools, allowing the productive ones to enter while diverting those that are less likely to contribute. In my career as an elementary school teacher I had a number of occasions in which I needed to politely filter out well-meaning offers from parents and community members who wanted to present on their favorite topic, which they knew my students "would just love to hear about." At the same time, my search beacon probed the community in search of relevant experts who could engage the kids at their level. Thus, I resisted esoteric lessons that were not connected to anything the kids were investigating (or, for that matter, even interested in), while at the same time I was negotiating with a local nature center to lower their age range for a bird-banding experience. I was intrigued with banding as a monitoring tool, and thought that it would extend the feeder-monitoring project sponsored by the Cornell Lab of Ornithology in which my third graders were participating. After some discussion (and likely my demonstration of persistence and seriousness of intent), we reached a compromise whereby the kids could observe the bird banding close at hand but they wouldn't hold the birds themselves. In this and many other instances of place-based education, the teacher needs to be an advocate for the students if they are to have more than packaged field trips.

Just as experts need to be filtered (both into and out of the educational landscape), a tool filter is needed to separate the productive tools from the latest over-marketed whiz-bang technology. Even though the tool may be potentially useful, if the learning curve is excessive compared with the benefits, looking for a simpler alternative is warranted. GIS software helped in making the tornado- and creek-monitoring projects meaningful, but I've seen other projects in which extensive and expensive technology is used for pedestrian purposes. It's far from uncommon in schools to see projects on the wall such as printouts of PowerPoint slides containing ersatz art or brief writings like haiku. As anyone who has attended a conference knows, PowerPoint is not an artistic medium, and I have to be skeptical that kids spending an entire period typing 17 syllables they had already written longhand is the best use of their time or the school's technology investment. From what I have observed, most computer lab writing time is spent choosing a font and a text color. Yet projects like these are no doubt justified by some as a kid-friendly exercise in preparing them to use as an essential business tool for their future life. Filtering the outside world to bring in needed expertise and tools and avoiding the siren song of technology for its own sake are essential components of expanding and protecting students' learning space. Many things are important, but you can't do everything. Elegance in teaching—as in other endeavors—requires choices, with a judicious use of subtraction as teachers work to get down to the essence of things (May, 2010). Filters are essential in this decision-making process.

In addition to Luckin's (2010) "people and tools" category, teachers need to consider several dimensions of the environment in which they teach. Specifically, the physical and cultural environment in the neighborhood may present certain opportunities or affordances that can't be realized in the classroom or school building. Also, the professional environment of the school can serve to enable or constrain adventurous teaching. We'll consider each of these factors in turn. First, the physical and cultural resources available in the neighborhood should factor quite a bit into teachers' decision making as they plan their curriculum. Teachers with the highest levels of agency have an uncanny ability to find and make use of these resources in ways that their less active colleagues don't. In an era of standardized, corporate-produced curriculum, these local flavors add life to the curriculum. More generally, getting kids out into the real world beyond the classroom is essential for their growth. Without these experiences, the classroom can become an insular space detached from the rest of the world. As Vascerello (2011) so eloquently puts it:

> The ventures outward enable children to build a concept of the world based on their own unfiltered experience—not someone else's—and offer the basis for forming opinions, sharing their opinions, modifying and enlarging their thinking based on the ideas and opinions of others. Through the emotional connections to the people and places children encounter . . . the children become participants in an ever-enlarging world and develop a sense of responsibility toward that world. (p. 155)

If teachers can make productive use of the learning spaces they find beyond the school—such as a nearby nature reserve or a historic neighborhood—this opens many doors for productive inquiry. Still, simple proximity isn't enough. Recalling Gresalfi and colleagues' research on how teachers use materials, the potential value of the site won't be realized if there are no intentions to use it well, or if the teachers lack the capacities needed to make good use of it. The school where I had my professional internship was adjacent to an environmental center, which supported many cross-curricular projects ranging from artistic sketches to scientific investigations. No doubt these early experiences in my career helped plant seeds for my later interest in place-based education. Each of the place-based projects noted here and those described elsewhere in the literature serve as examples of a teacher getting out, finding a space, and making use of it. Much of the work my staff and I do is serving as a coach for teachers in how to see the school grounds and the neighborhood and how to make effective use of what is there. This isn't always easy, as many suburban schools are segregated from much that is of ecological or cultural interest in the community. All too often, our after-school programs struggled to find meaningful project sites in close proximity to the school. Spending more than half the weekly program time in transportation to and from a research site isn't usually a good option.

Even when the affordances of a neighborhood can enable great projects, it's important to recognize that many urban schools have very real safety concerns that need to be considered. We've worked with several after-school programs that were restricted to working in the building or in areas immediately outside the building. As urban sites, these were inevitably mostly paved spaces and thus not all that interesting ecologically. While there were parks nearby, gang turf considerations created the perception that it was too dangerous to go into the community in which the kids lived. In partial defense of this reasoning, since some of the programs involved use of then-trendy GPS units, part of the concern was whether the kids were being set up as targets walking in the neighborhood with electronic regalia. Still, the constraint was in place regardless of whether the kids were to have the GPS equipment with them or not. Whether these threats were real is a somewhat secondary consideration. The perception was sufficient to lead to policies that constrained the students' options. As an outsider in the community, I was not equipped to filter the signals and contribute to the decision making, and thus had to rely on the site administrator's judgment. Still it's a sobering thought that the accepted view was that students can't investigate safely under a teacher's watch in their own community.

Throughout the decision-making process, teachers' knowledge of the local community is essential. They need to know what is available, how to access it, and how to leverage resources to extend students' learning. Over time, teachers can become invested in the school community, but it helps when it is not a solitary endeavor. Collegial sharing and support can help everyone move forward in using the local environment. Unfortunately, professional cultures founded on collaborative planning and sharing innovation are all too rare in schools, and it seems that they are getting rarer as professional discourse moves increasingly toward pacing charts and test scores. Over the 15 years I have worked for the Missouri Botanical Garden, participation in professional development workshops at our sites and at sites from similar cultural institutions in the area has declined significantly, to about half of what it used to be. When asked, teachers say regretfully that they simply don't have time in the curriculum for interesting projects since they "have so much to cover." Even among the adventurous teachers in our workshops, the discussion all too often reverts to meeting the standards rather than meeting the kids' needs. Be sure you have met your DOKs and your ILCs. When the discussion goes this way, I feel like I need to find my decoder ring.

Given this all too often rather barren collegial context, it is a very fortunate school that has been able to maintain a productive professional learning environment, where teachers share resources freely and support and challenge each other on the way toward improved practice. All too many schools are characterized by isolation, with each teacher working in his or her own rabbit hole, coming out only to eat a quick lunch and cover recess and dismissal duties. Obviously a collegial environment is more productive, assuming of course that the sharing is consistent with overarching goals of student autonomy and inquiry. Sharing pedagogically unproductive strategies ("Here's another fun worksheet to keep the kids busy when they finish their assignment") won't enhance the learning environment, and in fact serves to reinforce an approach to education that is counter to the authenticity sought by place-based and other progressive educators. Both the existence of the collegial pipeline and the pedagogic vision informing the content flowing through the pipe are important. The best teachers work from a strong, pedagogically grounded base but are also open to new perspectives that enhance their practice. Other teachers exhibit levels of passivity and/or defensiveness, either reacting simply to provide token compliance with administrative mandates about the "new" way to do things, or seeking to protect the status quo at all costs. "Close the door and leave me alone" is an unfortunate but all too common teaching strategy. At times, it's needed to protect what is good from outside interference, but it does limit the potential for good ideas to flow from a pioneering classroom to affect the fabric of the school culture.

This hope for the spread of innovation may be overly optimistic, of course. As we have seen throughout the book, changes that don't mesh with the pedagogic visions of the teachers and the system as a whole have a hard time taking root. Instead, the system tends to protect itself and its ways of doing things. In a couple of schools I worked at when I was a teacher, the clear goal among the faculty was either to "get to" the new teachers quickly to show how things were done there before any new ideas took root, or simply to let each teacher do what he or she wanted. At no point was there consideration that new faculty could bring ideas that would enrich the school. In one, the administration admitted that hiring mid-career teachers created a real management conundrum, since it was easier in terms of maintaining a uniform culture to hire less experienced and more malleable teachers. Ideally, teachers work in a collegial environment in which they share best practices founded on a common epistemic vision, make good use of community resources, and share insights into how individual students learn, leading jointly to better practice. Sadly, this Utopian ideal is rarely realized.

Throughout this chapter I've tried to show how professional agency and a shared collegial vision can enable more successful community engagement. An important factor in whether this is realized is the extent to which administrators either promote or suppress innovation and creativity among the faculty. Principals who embrace teacher and student ownership of learning can clear obstacles placed in the way by central administrators and overly concerned parents. Or, they can set up roadblocks seemingly at every turn. When every act of professional judgment requires prior authorization or documentation of the exception to plan, the bureaucratic overhead makes dynamic teaching—which by definition needs to be responsive to emerging opportunities—challenging to say the least. Given this potential for good or for harm, Luckin's (2010) concept of filters applies here as well. In a school with strong leadership, teachers can filter the administrators in, keeping them in the loop and using them as a sounding board for emerging ideas and as an ambassador to promote what is happening to parents and the community at large. Unfortunately, as principal roles shift toward management and away from the historical ideal of being the principal educator in the school, too many teachers need to engage in subterfuge as they filter out bureaucratic interference to protect student learning opportunities.

Summarizing the chapter as a whole, teachers with high levels of agency make decisions that are informed by a well-thought-out vision of learning and that draw from a base of understanding developed through reflection on previous experiences. These teachers also don't function in a vacuum. Rather, they leverage their own skills as well as those of their students, draw from a range of tools and people in the community, and make effective use of the physical, cultural, and collegial environment in which they work. Teachers exhibiting less professional agency rely on more scripted, formulaic learning experiences that tend not to foster the same level of student engagement. Both teacher and student slip into robot mode. The next chapter looks at these issues in more depth, considering how differences in the way teachers frame their work might explain variations in their degree of agency. In turn, this framing guides the many large and small decisions teachers make.

CHAPTER 4

Planning for Place-Based Learning

In the previous chapter, we saw how teachers go about making the many decisions that together constitute professional practice. To the extent that they don't just defer to a script, teachers make decisions that are informed by an effort to resolve a situation before them. These decisions draw from a forward-looking projection of what successful learning looks like and from a re-visioning of past experience. We also saw how these decisions are influenced (and to some extent bound) by such entities as tools, people, and environments.

In this chapter, we will look at specific design parameters that give shape to the plans that result from these decisions. First, we will start with a short overview contrasting the larger goal of authentic meaning underlying place-based education with some of the less useful approaches to meaning typically found in school. Following from there, we will look at ways in which teachers operating from different pedagogic frameworks use resources differently. Here we unpack more fully the work of Melissa Gresalfi and her colleagues (2012), which has been touched on a few times previously. Next, we'll see how these differences are in large part driven by more or less nuanced understandings of epistemology, or visions of how people learn. Effective place-based education and other educational strategies built on authentic meaning rely on a complex view of knowledge construction that isn't content to rely on fact nuggets and broad truisms. This is a fundamental but often overlooked difference between place-based and traditional education.

The second half of the chapter draws on these ideas and what has come before in articulating a generalized set of four design principles that we've seen built into the foundation of successful place-based projects. For a quick preview, we have found that successful projects are built on ambitious learning goals, use experience to help students build evidence and justifications, develop shared ownership among teachers and students, and involve sophisticated navigation of community resources. The chapter closes with comments on designing for student engagement, a process that starts to integrate the themes brought forth throughout the book.

To start, what does (or should) school look like? There are at least three major characterizations of school experiences worth considering. These are admittedly straw-person constructions, but they are useful in delineating some of the territory. Any real educational setting (whether in-school or after-school) will usually display at least an implicit preference for one of these constructions over the others, with aspects of each showing up in varying degrees in the overall curriculum plan.

Accumulating knowledge and skills for the future: In this construction—by far the dominant one in schools within the United States—the primary effort is focused on developing students' skills, knowledge, and worldview for future use. In many ways it echoes what Friere (1993) described as a "banking" approach to education, in which students are primed to accumulate what they need for envisioned future roles. "Do well in school so you can get a good job someday" is the prevailing ethic here. There are at least two sub-flavors of this approach, including a classical liberal arts education and a more modernistic one focused on preparing students for a future career in a STEM (science, technology, engineering, math) field. In both, the dominant effort for teachers is to cover vast curriculum areas with only occasional—and often contrived—efforts toward application. While this banking focus may not be intentional, it is a logical outcome of the way this future-focused paradigm works. As Laurillard (2012) notes, "The perceived need for education to deliver the curriculum . . . has tended to bias the teacher's interest toward acquisition rather than inquiry learning, leaving the student to discover these [inquiry] skills themselves; or not, as often happens" (p. 123).

In work that is framed by this construction students nominally learn a lot, but they don't necessarily have the ability to use what they have learned in any meaningful way, nor does it automatically lead to future learning capability. Recall and recitation are favored over sense-making and use of what is being learned. For example, it's common for elementary students we work with to learn about "regions." In practice, this all too often amounts to a textbook recitation of what region we live in, with at times absurd generalizations. For example, a dominant elementary textbook series helps students become well schooled in the (purported) cultural and ecological similarities of West Virginia and Florida, since both are listed in the same "southeast" region of the United States in their textbook. One of the great losses in a banking model of education is how little time is spent investigating the underlying model that dubiously tries to link an Appalachian coal-mining region with the Everglades in southern Florida. Students don't have opportunities to question in what ways the regions might be related, and in what ways other groupings might make more sense.

Acting out roles: This paradigm places some value on students' active engagement in projects, rather than their being in the passive "acquisition" mode just described. For this movement out of the textbook, teachers choosing this path should be lauded. For example, rather than simply reading about water quality and its importance, students in these classes will go out to the local creek or pond and collect data on relevant factors (e.g., pH, dissolved oxygen, and turbidity). This engagement with a somewhat authentic task also has the potential to support interdisciplinary investigations, so students in this hypothetical water investigation can also develop their data analysis and language skills as they interpret their findings. With the right supporting framework, students can develop a good, data-informed understanding of the underlying concepts. Given the higher level of activity, students are also likely to find this approach more engaging than a purely academic one, which has a risk of being rather dry.

What is lacking in an activity context—and which the next paradigm has the potential to address—is the usefulness of the students' efforts. The data collection and analysis effort might have served to address an academic goal, but without a defining purpose the fieldwork has no "legs" in that it doesn't go anywhere: Students don't take action on their results or use the results to build real understanding. For example, a common activity teachers want to do at our ecology center is to compare conditions in the prairie and the woodland. (Our location in eastern Missouri enables us to support both as functioning ecosystems.) As an activity, this is all to the good. As with the creek project just described, there is solid potential for building data collection skills and having discussions about the data. What limits the value here is the number of idiosyncrasies contained within the data collected on a given day. Within the same week we may get a quite different set of weather conditions, which has an impact on what data the kids collect. On sunny days there is a much more pronounced temperature difference between prairie and woodland than we see on cloudy days since the tree canopy provides some shielding that isn't present in the prairie. Also, this difference is only moderate at best in the early spring before the trees leaf out and provide the canopy cover that shades the woodland. To assert that one day's data are representative of "life in the woodlands" or "life in the prairie" is an overstatement to put it mildly.

Again, there is activity, which is laudable, but limited value comes from its largely context-free nature. Too much premium is placed on the activity itself (acting as scientists), not the outcome. Previous research has shown a tendency for teacher involvement in many citizen science projects to be more focused on activity than meaning. Looking across many projects, two former colleagues and I (Feldman, Konold, & Coulter, 2000) found that all too often teachers and students collected the data for the citizen science project but never returned to make use of the composite data sets that would place their local data in context. The activity was there ("We're participating in Project X . . ."), but the opportunity for greater meaning was missed. Note that this research was done before the time crunch that teachers now face in our current era of standardized, test-driven accountability. It's likely even harder now for many teachers to make use of these larger, context-building data sets.

It should also be noted that in some cases student activity can be nothing more than an engagement hook lacking academic substance. While there are certainly more activities in school like the data collection efforts just described—well-intended but not fully articulated—there are plenty of activities that are just pretending to be learning focused. We need to name these for what they are, since kids deserve better. In these cases, students will have an exciting but academically vacuous experience. Weather-focused programs that set kids up to be weathercasters parroting a forecast do little to help in learning about weather concepts. The effort becomes essentially a science-themed drama exercise. Also, we can safely put most diorama and poster-making activities in this category: activities to put a crafty spin on facts passed along without much digestion. We need a richer theory of action if we are to avoid activity-mania.

Learning for authentic purposes: The third construction builds on the ones just described, in that students do get out in the community to pursue authentic tasks and engage with academically substantive concepts. The key difference here is that the work is premised on knowledge and activity, but it goes further by making a difference through meaningful engagement. Thus, the experience is not limited to using an activity simply as a training ground for potentially useful future skills or as a means to apply concepts being learned. (Still worse from a design point of view are the activities done just to keep the class from getting too boring.) Instead, here the emphasis is on learning and acting for a real purpose, and not accumulating facts and ideas "just in case you ever need it." To continue the water-monitoring example, we've worked with students who go beyond the data collection effort, using it to inform a community education effort about clean water. Also, as noted in Chapter 1, a few years ago we worked with a school in a community with a military base that was producing a guide to the community for the high number of families moving in as part of a tour of duty. In both cases, there was a purpose beyond the academic task, real roles for students to take on, and a lasting value for people outside of the class. Classes that work from this paradigm embody Dewey's premise, cited earlier, that education should be about life, not a preparation for a future life. There is also a more robust concept of experience at work here, going beyond the overly simplistic idea that experience is just "what kids do." Rather, echoing Dewey (1938a/1963), to be an experience in this context means to take on a problematic situation and work diligently to its resolution. Only when the resolution has been achieved in the learner's mind can you say that the student has had an educative experience.

While there is a considerable "upside" to this approach, it has the significant logistical drawback of being rather time consuming for the teacher and requiring considerable agency on the part of both the teachers and students. Everyone involved needs to take risks and break out of the business-as-usual banking paradigm of schooling. Needless to say, few school systems reward this kind of initiative, so the default teacher role is by far the easier one to assume. Pragmatically speaking, for teachers to frame all of their curriculum within this construction would require super-human initiative. Still, this is where the payoff is, making it imperative that we work toward a greater portion of a student's learning experience being based on this more educationally engaging paradigm. Learning that is anchored in fully authentic purposes will never characterize 100% of a school curriculum, but every move away from facts for their own sake and toward greater meaning is a victory.

Charting a path forward, we need to support teachers in using elements of each framing—knowledge, activity, and purpose—building toward a productive synthesis that values robust conceptual development experiences. Through these experiences, students can see future professional options, and have opportunities today to apply what is being learned in ways that are valued by the students and by the community. Viewing the contemporary educational landscape in the United States and in many other countries, adding more lectures and readings isn't the highest need. Banking-oriented, future-focused education is already by far the norm, sanctioned by district curriculum guides and assessment schemes. Rather, greater emphasis needs to be placed on students building capacity and engagement by taking on and sustaining a range of authentic and semi-authentic tasks that build cognitive and affective engagement. The more "real" we can make students' experiences, the more they will see the value of the knowledge and skills that are otherwise being banked for some undefined future use. To use a basketball analogy, players are more likely to practice free throws after they see how those points can make a crucial difference in a close game. Without a purpose, endless skill practice done for its own sake rapidly loses interest. Since most school curriculum never gets off the practice court, so to speak, students' persistent disaffection with school (Yazzie-Mintz, 2010) should not be surprising.

The practical implications of how teachers' define their roles can be made more tangible by using a framework developed by Melissa Gresalfi and her colleagues (Gresalfi, Barnes, & Cross, 2012). In it, she draws on ecological psychology to describe how teachers with different orientations toward project-based learning (and thus, different pedagogic frames) make different uses of the same district-chosen, project-based curriculum materials. In her research, a more traditionally oriented teacher was observed to emphasize mastery of procedural knowledge with his students, whereas a second teacher who was more focused on project-based learning engaged her students in a broader range of knowledge. What was particularly striking was how students in the first class (with the more traditional teacher) were much more likely than students in the other class to respond to higher-level question prompts from the curriculum with procedural- and factual-level responses. Based on their previous experience of what the class is about (and perhaps the teacher's implicit clues), the students in the traditionally framed class were more likely to meet the teacher's norms and downshift the questions toward rote learning. Conversely, students in the class led by a teacher who already possessed a professional disposition to support project-based learning (and thus didn't just have it imposed by external fiat) engaged more fully and creatively with the curriculum. The students' understanding of classroom norms led to a higher level of participation and discourse, and didn't lead them to downshift their engagement. Thus, we see how teachers' frames of teaching and learning can have a tangible impact on students' own frames, and in turn on how they experience what are nominally the same materials.

Interpreting her data, Gresalfi (2012) argues that "what happens in any particular moment is based on a co-constructed set of possible actions defined by (1) the affordances of the environment for a particular action, (2) the intention of the agent to take up those affordances, and (3) the effectivities of the agent to actually realize those affordances" (p. 250). There is a lot of academic phrasing here, so let's unpack these terms:

Affordances are simply what is made possible by the materials available. As Gresalfi notes, a chair is good for sitting; a door is not. In terms of curriculum, materials have a way of favoring certain approaches to learning. A traditional textbook has affordances that support acquisition learning, with students receiving packaged information. An activity guide like one of the classic Elementary Science Study (ESS) modules has the affordance of supporting open-ended inquiry. Each resource has a role, whether it be to provide scientific information or to promote an investigative mindset. The important element here is that not all resources are the same. By design, each has certain affordances that make some uses more likely than others. Yes, you can sit on a door instead of a chair, and formulaic textbooks can support inquiry,[1] but in both cases they are being used for purposes that are somewhat counter to what they were designed for. Usable in a pinch, but not ideal.

Intentions are pretty much as you would expect: What does the teacher intend for the activity to look like in practice, and in turn what are the students' intentions for engaging in the activity put before them? In Gresalfi's study (and in my experience over the past decade in leading an ecology center), the intentions held by a teacher are critical. Classes working at our ecology center most

---

[1] For example, early in my teaching career we used the official science textbooks to prop up boards on which we were building marble courses, and as standardized weights to test bridge constructions made out of newspaper.

often split into groups of four to six students, each of which is led by a volunteer whom we have trained in natural history and pedagogy, and who is nominally pursuing the same goals for the field experience. Even within this structure, though, it is more the norm than the exception for group leaders to vary quite a bit in their underlying pedagogic intentions. Some will lead the students in open-ended, student-driven exploration, responding to kids' questions and occasionally pointing out particularly intriguing features. Others working from a "transmission" frame of teaching tend to focus on providing full and scientifically accurate explanations of what the students are seeing. In essence, the focus is on things the kids need to know. Thus, even with the same resources at hand (immediate access to bottomland forest and prairie ecosystems, as well as a variety of field guides and investigative tools), group leaders with different teaching intentions create different learning experiences for the students.

Effectivities also play into this model, as they describe a person's ability to make use of what is before them. Even if the tools have the necessary affordances to support my work, and my intentions are closely aligned with what the materials make possible (the affordances), I still need to be able to know how to use them. Teachers and students can be trained in fairly short order on the use of fairly simple tools such as rain gauges and GPS receivers. More complex tools and tasks require a greater learning investment before a sufficient level of effectivity can be realized. This is true both for advanced investigative tools like geographic information system (GIS) software and for more complex pedagogical techniques such as leading rich, data-informed discussions with students. For these, a greater investment of time is essential if a reasonable degree of fluency in using the tools is to be achieved. This capacity dimension is critical: A resource-rich learning environment that offers great affordances and that is led by a teacher with the best of intentions is not enough. Without effectivity, or being able to *use* what is available, successful learning and engagement will be limited.

If we accept these dimensions of Gresalfi's framework as being important, it should be clear that all three need a level of synchronicity for effective learning to take place. Limitations in any of them will limit the overall success of the endeavor. Material selection processes at all levels from the state- and district-level selection of textbooks, curriculum plans, and assessment tools down to the specific items used in a local classroom on a given day will show a bias in favor of certain approaches over others. Using the budget to buy textbooks supports a different approach to learning than does purchase of field kits. The affordances of each choice will enable or constrain different learning options. Similarly, intentions regarding how to use the materials and how to structure the class serve to put bounds on what happens with students. Teachers who head out into the field intending to convey information to their students create experiences with a very different slant than do those who go out with an exploratory mindset. Each is working from a different frame of what their task is, which leads to different intentions. Finally, skill or effectivity matters. Creating active, engaged classes won't happen without the requisite pedagogic skills for managing groups, leading discussions, and linking with community resources. Content understanding is also important: You need to know enough natural or local history to know what is of most value in structuring an investigation.

While the focus in this chapter is on teachers, a parallel argument can be drawn for students, at least as far as intentions and effectivities are concerned. The intentions they bring to the task help to define the experience. Choices of whether to engage in the tasks at hand or to remain passive, whether to collaborate with peers or remain isolated (or be disruptive) all factor into the success of a project. Similarly, the students' effectivities matter. If they can't measure the data reliably that is needed for a project, the value of the data will be compromised. In turn, this undermines the project as a whole. Still, it pays to keep in mind the research by Gresalfi (2012) showing how students respond to different teaching styles. It would be unfair to park all of the responsibility on teachers, but as the adults (and trained professionals) in the relationship, they have to bear the disproportionate responsibility.

As should be clear by now, teachers' choices and capacities matter for student learning. While this statement is in some respects self-evident, the preceding analysis goes further than standard considerations of effective teaching to consider how role framing influences (and perhaps even determines) notions of professional competence. Unfortunately, these nuances are lost in calls made by politicians to base measures of teacher competency on simple and marginally valuable measures such as student test scores. As we have seen in the previous chapter and this one, effective teaching requires much more judgment than these calls for shallow measures allow for.

Thinking about Complex Thinking: Epistemology and Place-Based Education

In the overview of the agency model described in the previous chapter, differences in epistemology, or how we see learning and the process of coming to know, were alluded to briefly. At that point, it was enough to acknowledge that teachers' visions of successful learning will be different based on whether they see knowledge as a set of facts and processes for students to accumulate, or as a complex and tentative web of understandings to be constructed over time. Looking specifically toward a successful place-based program, however, this latter view of knowledge must take hold. Overreliance on accumulating fixed-form knowledge is of limited value for place-based and other authentic learning environments since "fact nuggets" devoid of context are usually too general in scope and wrapped in a finality of sorts that doesn't easily support building conceptual linkages. Something more is required, which is why place-based educators tend to have a fairly complex vision of what useful knowledge is. To make sense of this, we need to delve into the abstract but fascinating realm of personal epistemology.

In their overview of personal epistemology, Feucht and Bendixen (2010) summarize a number of overlapping paradigms currently at work in the field. There are some who propose a developmental continuum, with learners starting with an initial state of holding (and relying on) fixed, absolute forms of knowledge. Over time and with the right support, people can move toward being able to use more contingent, relative models that are either context-specific (e.g., distinctively historical or scientific ways of knowing), or that take a more general view of seeing all knowledge as being subject to inherent limits in our ability to define anything with absolute certainty. In this latter framing of knowledge as a set of tentative propositions, the best we can hope for is to construct provisional beliefs that are underwritten by sufficient justification to be relied on. While there are variations in each "continuum" model, when taken together these frameworks of personal epistemology assume a general trajectory from lesser to more complex understandings of knowledge as a learner matures. For the most part, teachers are likely to embrace this view of epistemology, but it is an open question how much of this more complex thinking on the far end of the trajectory shows up in a typical student's daily work.

Complementing these generalized, trajectory-based epistemological frameworks, there are other, more nuanced models that seek to articulate specific dimensions of personal epistemology, not just a general trend toward appreciating greater complexity in what counts as knowledge. For example, Schommer-Aikens (2002, pp. 104–105) describes five key dimensions of personal epistemology:

1. *The structure of knowledge:* Whether knowledge exists in separate chunks (or nuggets as I described them earlier).
2. *The stability of knowledge:* The extent to which knowledge is persistent and unchanging, or subject to modification over time in light of new understandings and/or new evidence.
3. *The source of knowledge:* The balance of authority, reasoning, and first-hand experience.
4. *The speed of learning:* Whether learning is a question of simply "getting it" or not, or if it is something that can be developed over time with persistent effort.

5. *The ability to learn:* Related to the previous point, whether learning is an "innate ability" or something that most anyone can do.

To make these parameters more tangible, let's apply them to the fifth grade native plant garden project introduced in Chapter 1 as an example. In terms of structure, knowledge in this project is constructed as a complex web of ideas, in which the kids have to integrate a range of information about individual plants and the growing conditions in and near the garden. Stability of knowledge is tentative, subject to modification as the results come in showing whether the plants thrive or not in their chosen locations. If not, the students may need to re-think their plans. (In fact, students in the year following the initial planting had to do just that as they filled in bare spots in the garden where plants didn't make it.) More generally, students came to see knowledge as coming from a more diverse set of informants: Field guides, horticulture professionals, their teacher, and their own experience all came together to inform decisions and actions. As learners, their conceptual understanding grew through iterative experience that unfolded over time, rather than simply having a lesson and then having their mastery tested.

In reflecting on the merits of a more detailed epistemological framework compared with a general trajectory toward more sophisticated thought, Schommer-Aikens (2002) specifically considers the potential benefit to teachers. She argues that in being able to understand in more detail certain dimensions of how students think, teachers can respond more constructively than they might be able to with a more generalized construct. But this assumption of actual use value for teachers relies on the teacher recognizing the value of this diagnostic information, and being in a position to make use of it. Again, this is where scripted instruction and overly simple accountability data work against better understanding of how individual kids are learning, and how to help them develop capacity over time. Even if we accept Schommer-Aikens's framework as being potentially useful, for a teacher working in a delivery-focused, highly scripted teaching environment it is unlikely that the levels of interaction taking place will allow forms of epistemic complexity to rise to the surface. Rather, in the rush to coverage, nominal "understanding" is much more likely to be a matter of presenting the approved truths on cue.

There are, of course, exceptions to the rule as teachers work against the grain to create complex, dynamic learning spaces, but these pioneering efforts are not nearly as common as they need to be. This is particularly true in the realm of elementary school science, which has long been a point of concern in educational circles. Given that most elementary teachers are themselves poorly educated in the sciences, it becomes doubly hard to foster epistemically rich, complex thinking in students. The convergence of time pressure and a teacher's own relatively unsophisticated personal epistemology as it relates to science leads to textbook (and textbook-like) presentations of science. Reflecting on the role of textbook-style materials, Bell and Linn (2002) observe:

> When students follow a set protocol in order to replicate a well-established finding, they may come to believe that science consists of the simple, unproblematic unfolding of new information or "truths." These views are quite distant from the actual controversy that pervades much of the leading edge scientific research. Textbook accounts also often ignore the interpretive and conjectural dimensions associated with the development of new scientific knowledge. (p. 325)

The net result for community-based environmental projects is a real challenge: How can teachers who are—because of both personal and institutional factors—tied to finished, final-form understandings be expected to lead students into the messy world of real issues and competing claims that don't comport well with textbook explanations?

This consideration of teachers' ability to use epistemologically complex instruction is picked up by Bell and Linn (2002) in their investigations of how science teaching practices can support students' growth toward complex understandings of knowledge. They note that students all too often have difficulty in developing a coherent view of science, but that they benefit from opportunities to critique inquiry methods and scientific conclusions and to debate competing points of view. Bell and Linn go on to suggest that the difficulties students experience can be a by-product of their instructional environment, as these environments are often situations wherein "the development of science inquiry proceeds somewhat independently from the development of science disciplinary knowledge, [and thus] connections between inquiry and disciplinary understanding may remain weak" (p. 335). Fortunately, other research (e.g., Linn & Hsi, 2000) suggests that this inquiry–content gap can be mitigated when learning experiences are personally meaningful, as they presumably would be in a place-based program for which students had a suitable degree of ownership. Also, looking at specific instructional practices, Bell and Linn (2002) summarize research investigating the impact of instruction that specifically engaged eighth graders in thinking like scientists through analysis of controversies within the field. In that research, Bell documented three areas of student growth that were statistically significant: Understanding (1) that debate helps lead to improved ideas; (2) that judicious use of evidence helps to support argumentation; and (3) that debate helps in refining your own ideas. Each of these outcomes is practiced in a well-designed place-based project, and is clearly beneficial to students' ability to function effectively in taking on messy real-world problems. These are useful examples showing where a place-based approach can help to address core issues in science education.

Throughout their research, Bell, Linn, and Hsi scope out potential ways in which cognitively complex thinking *can* take place if the setting is right. It's important to remember, though, that the teacher is the one who is the final broker of the space in which these experiences happen. If the teacher doesn't have the time, autonomy, capacity, or inclination to support learning that builds epistemic capacity, it won't happen. Viewed more broadly, we have to acknowledge that despite our own biases there is no universally held "correct" way of thinking about how students should learn science. As we saw in Gresalfi's (2012) research (and was evident but less explicitly documented in many of our projects), some teachers prioritize certain goals over others, even if they are nominally teaching from the same materials.

Given this, we need to acknowledge just how central teachers' epistemic visions are to what they value educationally and in turn how these values impact decision making, both in the broad planning of learning experiences and in their everyday interactions with kids. In particular, reliance on terminology-laden textbooks that present science as a set of final truths favors a particular view of the structure and stability of knowledge. Related to this, the extent to which the text is seen as authoritative reflects an understanding of the source of knowledge being in external experts. Conversely, programs that rely on first-hand experience give primacy to sensory data as a source of knowledge. Both of these frameworks are limited, though, if students don't have opportunities to synthesize their understandings in a rich community of inquiry where points of view can be challenged and elaborated upon. Complementing these knowledge-focused beliefs, understandings of a learner's speed and ability to learn are reflected in the time allotted for conceptual development, and in the assumed level of students' ability. Rapid movement through a preset, strongly demarcated curriculum favors those who can engage in quick absorption and recall to the detriment of those with a more organic, emerging approach to learning. History is replete with examples of highly accomplished, deeply intellectual people who would likely have scored poorly on school measures requiring quick assimilation and recall on demand.

To summarize, these epistemic dimensions have a significant impact on defining a teacher's vision of effective teaching and learning. As Feucht and Bendixen (2010) note, drawing on terms developed by Kuhn and Weinstock (2002):

> Absolutist teachers may tend to perceive teaching as transferring knowledge from teachers as experts to students as naive and passive learners, while evaluativist teachers may promote learning activities in which students collaboratively construct knowledge and are expected to justify their knowledge. (p. 7)

Framing Teaching for Place-Based Education

Building on the premise that teaching is a highly complex undertaking, what are the implications for place-based education? How do teachers who craft rich, community-based learning projects see their jobs? What do they do differently in comparison with other teachers? To address these questions, we will look at four dimensions of practice characteristic of teachers who are successful in engaging their kids in meaningful place-based programs. Each of these factors was regularly at work in the more effective place-based programs we've worked with, and largely absent in the less successful programs despite the same resource supports and similar profiles of professional experience. In short, effective place-based teachers are expert in:

- Working toward ambitious goals
- Using experiences to assemble evidence and build justifications
- Building shared ownership with students
- Navigating community resources

Working toward ambitious goals

One of the hallmarks of teachers who are more successful in leading place-based programs (or, arguably, in most any other complex educational paradigm) is their determination to pursue ambitious goals with their students. To be clear, the term "ambition" here presumes a certain level of authentic engagement. Thus, it's more than just ramping the school game up a notch or two to be "accelerated." That's just labeling and wishful thinking that betray an underlying ignorance about the nature of real learning. Rather, ambition in this context means having kids engage with complex issues such as restoring native plant species and documenting the ecological impact of their work, or taking on real responsibilities by monitoring how traffic patterns impact local air pollution. The specific projects will have to match the experience base and developmental capacities of the students, but at any age there is a qualitative difference between these messy and complex—but ultimately meaningful—forms of engagement and the more pedestrian field trip model in which students go to "see" parts of the environment. As teachers and students pursue these ambitious goals, they may not achieve total success. For most real-world issues there is always something more that can be done. In the examples just mentioned, invasive species will creep back in, and the air quality will never be pristine. Still, students and teachers can celebrate successes along the way, whether that is seen in an increase in the number of pollinators recorded, or improved breathing space. The art form here is for teachers to craft a vision of students and community members working together toward ambitious, meaningful goals that have intermediate points of success that can be celebrated.

In addition to ambitious outcomes for community engagement, a parallel argument can be made for the teacher having ambitious pedagogic goals for students. Beyond good grades and high test scores, effective place-based teachers create spaces where students can take on the role of a science learner, using the work at hand as a means to build interest and skill. Over time this becomes a reflexive process in which each experience feeds the next, iteratively building curiosity, capacity, and commitment. Just as with the community impact goals, it is good for teachers to have support built into their designs both for relatively attainable learning goals that nearly all students will reach, as well as the depth of engagement that allows for some students to invest more effort and reach a higher level of "payoff." For example, a science teacher might want all of her students to find science meaningful and relevant, with the hope that some will go on to pursue STEM-related careers in the future. Thus, creating a scientific culture in the classroom that invites cognitive and affective engagement with science is a good starting point in that it will make the daily class experiences meaningful for most students. Realistically, the teacher has to assume varying degrees of engagement for individual students, and will need to be sure there are ample opportunities for those students who are currently disengaged with science to reconnect, as well as space for those who want to go further to build a deeper science interest and identity. These seeds planted by an effective teacher will emerge over time, leading some students toward considering future STEM-related career choices, with an even larger pool of students developing a more favorable disposition toward science. This consciously chosen pedagogic vision goes quite a bit beyond a more traditional model in which teachers simply hope that some will find science exciting and interesting if the class is fun enough. A suitably ambitious teacher will be able to scope out long-term content and pedagogy targets to be aimed for while simultaneously seeing interim points of success to be celebrated along the way. From these signposts, pathways can be designed to realize these targets.

Using experiences to assemble evidence and build justification

One of the fundamental differences we have found between teachers who are more or less successful in building place-based projects is the extent to which they use experiences to build a base of evidence, and in turn support students in using that evidence to build justifications for their understanding. This becomes quite apparent in mentoring teachers in their efforts to design fieldwork. By way of comparison, consider these two plans for field experiences sent to me by elementary grade teachers (coincidentally within the same week):

We've been talking about landforms we see in Missouri, fossils from Missouri . . .

And:

Perhaps the first method [of investigation] would be best if the goal is to record pollinator data. I will have to adjust for different grades. I could do different methods with different groups. I could also do some test runs with some students and see what works.

In the first example, it's indecipherable what goals the teacher (who I know has the best of intentions) has for learning outcomes, or even what she wants the kids to be doing in their field experience. Rather, the work is embedded in what is seemingly the universal verb for elementary grade science classes: *talk* (as in "We *talked* about . . . We're going to *talk* about . . ." etc.). The second quote reflects a teacher seeking help in developing a methodology to document the pollinator population attracted to the native plant garden that she and her students designed and built with our assistance. Her school is in a shared space with a local church, and she is responding to the church rector's concern about the appearance of the students' garden. Note the agency at work here: Rather than simply deferring to authority, the teacher wanted to be able to show the value of the space in terms of the ecosystem services it provides, and build students' inquiry and data analysis capacities in the process.

The contrast in the two plans is striking: In the first, there is a fairly general process of talking about phenomena that most of the students haven't experienced, leading to a field trip goal to see some of what they have been talking about. The field experience would be a modest upgrade, since "talk about" would become "see" and presumably make the phenomena more real for the kids. Still, there is very little in the way of actual science or other meaningful forms of experience on the agenda. The poverty of this approach is clear when it is compared with the second school, where there is a clear goal wrapped in a meaningful project, with an emphasis on students collecting data and using those data to build justified conclusions. In response to this gap, we have recently begun a campaign with teachers to "upgrade their verbs" in the interest of science. Sadly, progress has been limited. Professional frames are held tenaciously.

Building shared ownership with students

Contained within the pollinator example just cited and in many other place-based projects, there is a level of shared ownership between teachers and students (and quite often involving other members of the community as well). For the pollinator study, the students were being slated by the teacher to be involved in doing trial runs of the data collection, with a larger goal of working collaboratively with the students toward developing a scientifically valid monitoring protocol. More fundamentally, the teacher was inviting the students to document the ecological benefits of *their* garden—the one they helped to design and install, and the one that needed justification to an important stakeholder.

Contrast this with other garden projects we have worked with, where the first contact is typically an email from a teacher asking whether she could come by and pick up a garden's worth of plants to install. While there would be some level of activity going on if this plan were enacted (assuming of course that the kids would be doing the planting), there wouldn't be nearly the level of intention and ownership for the kids if the plants just showed up. Digging on command out in the courtyard might be a welcome break from the classroom, but it's hardly an educative experience. Where teachers are amenable to working with us to build a richer learning experience we try to slow the process down long enough to have the kids conduct research on a range of "candidate" plants we bring to the school. We also lead the kids out to the proposed planting site to model for the kids (and the teacher) how to assess the site. For example, if shade is likely to be an issue, we try to model a way to question and then investigate levels of sunlight, a key variable for the growth of plant species. Before we leave, we encourage the kids (in the presence of the teacher) to monitor the sunlight over the course of the school day, and to repeat this for a few days before we return to help them create their garden. In practice, this happens in some cases and sometimes it does not. When it does, the students are well on their way to a rich educative experience in which they can take on stewardship responsibility for their garden. If not, at least the kids did get out into the courtyard to do some planting, and they were able to exercise some degree of nurturing for a plant. To the teacher's credit, even in these more marginal efforts there was a degree of activity beyond the "talk," but it is still a long way from a planting activity to the shared ownership that is the hallmark of good place-based projects.

It is important to reiterate here that shared ownership does not have to be a fully equal partnership. A wise teacher always considers the students' capacities in making pedagogic decisions. Presumably a high school environmental science class will be able to take on more ownership for the design and implementation of a project than a kindergarten class would. Recalling the GIS-enhanced water-monitoring project involving a pair of fifth graders described in a previous chapter, this was a collaborative effort to choose monitoring sites, select the data tools and protocols, and locate community experts. As rather bright 10-year-old kids, the students had some capacity to contribute to the project design, but were hardly in a position to design and execute the project on their own. A good rule of thumb here might be for the teacher not to take over what the students can do for themselves, but to provide the guidance needed to extend students' own capacity. As Dewey (1938a/1963) reminds us, it's actually best practice for teachers to use their longer, richer life experience to guide students. Not doing so devalues the teacher's experience. Recalling the agency model from the last chapter, a good project is based on a well-crafted vision of successful outcomes, and draws from the teacher's and the students' experiences. Laissez-faire approaches that leave the students to their own devices in a misguided effort to give students ownership do them a disservice. But if we simply take over on the assumption that the students can't or won't do the work, it's no longer much of an educational project. As we saw in the earlier discussion of students' experiences, co-ownership between the teacher and students is an essential component of place-based projects.

Navigating community resources

The fourth hallmark of exemplary place-based practice is an ability to navigate community resources. Linking back to the discussion of Luckin's (2010) "ecology of resources" model in the previous chapter, more effective teachers have the pedagogic sense of which resources—human, physical, and virtual—will contribute to a strong project. Equally important, they know how to navigate the process of getting those resources lined up for productive student use. Examples of this include the teacher cited earlier leading his fourth graders in an investigation of access to healthy food in the community, who found a local retailer who came to be interviewed by the students. Likewise, a middle school developing an outdoor classroom rich with native plants connected with a local Boy Scout needing a location for his Eagle Scout project. That space now has a nice set of teen-built benches adding considerable functionality to the outdoor classroom. The same school tapped internal expertise, using the industrial arts teacher for some of the design projects, and the math teacher to help the students in laying out an outdoor game board.

In each of these cases, rather than being wrapped up in a race for "covering the curriculum," the teacher was able to maintain a dual focus, looking deeply at the needs for the project at hand and at the same time scanning the community to see what resources were out there that could contribute to the students' learning experiences. All of this work, of course, is done on the base of a strong understanding of the kids' interests, capacities, and needs. As teachers make the many decisions that go into designing for a strong educational experience, informed judgment and resourcefulness become critically important. Hence, there is the need for agency among teachers pursuing place-based projects. Cheerful robots can't do this work.

The challenge for improving education is that relatively few teachers are able to frame their work in this way, operating as they do in a long-standing system that doesn't encourage, reward, or even allow this type of role definition. If you recall the split among teacher identities described at the outset, some take a more active approach in sculpting the learning environment, while others are more passive in complying with scripted plans. They will of course tinker around the edges to make the classroom a more humane space for their students, but by and large they don't engage in fundamental rethinking of the classroom dynamics. To build strong, place-based programs we need more teachers who act with an eye toward exploiting possibilities—since these are the ones who will be able to create dynamic and engaging learning environments. As Erving Goffman (1986) notes:

> In our society we feel that intelligent agents have the capacity to gear into the ongoing natural world and exploit its determinacy . . . . Moreover, it is felt that . . . whatever an agent seeks to do will be continuously conditioned by natural constraints, and that effective doing will require the exploitation, not the neglect, of this condition. (p. 23)

Schools tend to be highly structured, often intransigent environments when it comes to any but the smallest of details. Thus, a teacher committed to an active place-based program will need to "gear into it" and exploit what is available in the school and community to achieve his pedagogic ends. A certain level of stoic pragmatism is required, accepting the limits of the situation but always looking for what is possible (Lachs, 2012). Even the most capable teacher won't be able to control everything, but his choices will—he hopes—move the learning situation closer to his desired state. Within every place-based teacher you will find a ray of optimism that sustains the effort.

Designing for Engagement

As we have seen over the course of this chapter and the previous one, teachers who go beyond the script do so because of a particular role framing they have for themselves and their students. Since they aren't comfortable basing their practice on more typically scripted pedagogic norms, they tend to work beyond using standard textbooks and pacing charts to determine their course of action. Given this disposition to chart a new course beyond what is given to them, place-based teachers and others seeking to create a more complex learning environment take on a design role as they craft student experiences. To bring this consideration of teachers' choices to a close, let's take a look at what this design process entails and what sorts of experiences are given priority.

Building from the earlier discussion of the need for knowledge and action to be pursued not for their own sake, but rather in a way that is motivated by authentic purposes, there are specific design features that need to be woven into the fabric of these pursuits. Laurillard (2012, p. 103, emphasis in the original) summarizes this quite well when she posits that the overarching intention of teachers' learning designs should be to "*motivate* or *enable* the learner to *generate* their *articulations* and *actions* that *modulate* their *concepts* and *practice.*" Throughout, the teacher sparks the student as the generator of ideas. These ideas in turn are modulated and extended by peer and teacher feedback and further experience. As a classroom shifts toward these goals, it moves away from the traditional IRE (initiate, respond, evaluate) framework wherein the teacher initiates a question, the student responds, and the teacher evaluates the response. This IRE learning script has a tenacious hold on schools, only being lightly mitigated in more student-friendly classrooms where kids are nominally free to do their work within bounds and spaces determined by the teacher. Even with some spatial freedom to work in the corner or at an activity table, the tasks themselves all too often remain deeply rooted in the IRE mindset in which the teacher is the initiator of the question and the only real evaluator of the response, the Alpha and the Omega, if you will.

While remaining mindful that the teacher as the most experienced and professionally trained member of the group needs to remain the architect of the learning environment, the tasks need to shift away from the traditional IRE model toward a more interactive mesh of experiences that benefit from student initiation, response, and evaluation. In this setting the teacher becomes the senior learning partner more than the sole source of authority in the classroom. From the student's point of view, the tasks take on a broader range of options. Laurillard (2012) articulates six processes that serve to illustrate this more complex engagement quite nicely: acquisition, inquiry, practice, production, discussion, and collaboration. Complementing this, Laurillard also offers a set of teacher and peer cycles focusing on communication, practice, and modeling that serve to shift the authority structure toward a shared venture. In essence, the IRE script is inverted, with each learner individually and in work groups expected to initiate ideas, gain responses from peers, teachers, and others as available, and evaluate the feedback received.

Throughout, there is a level of task complexity that represents a significant movement forward in terms of how it invites and holds students' cognitive and affective engagement. While drawing from the mathematics education context, there is much that place-based educators can learn from the Mathematical Task Framework developed by the QUASAR group at the University of Pittsburgh (Stein, Smith, Henningsen, & Silver, 2009). There, they articulate two critical distinctions: First, between tasks that are *by design* cognitively high or low, and second, between tasks that are *intended to be implemented at a high level* but that in the process of being implemented get downshifted by the teacher to a lower level. An example of this is the teacher Gresalfi (2012) was researching who took a complex problem-based learning curriculum and managed to downshift the students' experiences into a more prosaic level of activity. For the tasks themselves, Stein and colleagues (2009, pp. xvi–xvii) offer the contrast between a simple calculation problem in which given the dimensions of a room, students need to calculate how much carpet is needed, and a more complex problem seeking to optimize the space that could be made for a rabbit enclosure given a certain amount of fencing. On the one hand, the official curriculum checklist can be addressed just the same with either problem. Both involve building nominal facility with basic elementary school geometry computations. On the other hand, though, in terms of the underlying learning there is a world of difference between everyone pursuing the same calculation and being graded on its accuracy, and the creative cognitive space that is offered by the search for optimization embedded in the second option.

Returning to Laurillard's (2012) processes, students pursuing the space optimization challenge have real opportunities for acquisition of information, goal-focused inquiry, practice of basic skills, production of results (such as a table of different options and a theory of how to optimize results), discussion among peers and with the teacher, and meaningful collaboration. Along with the move toward this more complex task, there is an impetus toward higher-level thinking and engagement. To realize this, it is important that the task not be downshifted toward simplicity. As we saw earlier in Gresalfi's (2012) research, the same materials can be implemented in different ways. Whether through the teacher's discomfort with higher-level inquiry or through an economization driven by time constraints, implementation choices can strip complex tasks of much of their value. We need to keep the learning complex.

So what does all of this have to do with designing place-based education? Quite simply, everything. Effective place-based education projects need to keep the ownership shared, inverting the traditional IRE framework to prioritize students' initiation of tasks as much as developmentally possible. With this, teachers as the group leaders need to embrace the messy complexity of real-world problems, not shield their students from it. Tasks need to stay in the zone of proximal development, challenging but able to be reached with the assistance of the teacher, peers, and community members who can scaffold the learning as needed. Local history needs to stay closer to GIS-enhanced investigations of changing community demographics and away from the photocopied and mounted (yet unread) local history texts. Environmental studies need to focus on making sense of environmental impacts on water quality and away from one-off data collection trips. When teachers and others who are responsible for instructional design are able to do this, they can avoid the mind-numbing homogenization that is all too present in schools today. Dewey (1934/2005) advocates for an aesthetic appeal that motivates learners and invites participation. All too often, school provides an anesthetic numbing function for teachers and students alike.

To remedy this, we all need to work toward changing the system to enable great teaching to flourish. As the front-line professionals in this, teachers need to be sure they are exercising as much agency as they can to create engaging, developmentally sound, and intellectually complex learning spaces. Drawing on the elements introduced in this chapter, these project designs need to exploit the affordances available, invite intentional use, and build everyone's capacity. All of this effort needs to be pointed toward building complex understanding, not just focused on an accumulation of facts for rapid recall on demand. Throughout, students need to be the ones generating and (with the teacher's guidance) critiquing work products. Because of the general lack of institutional support for these pedagogic goals, this effort will by and large require freelance design either by sole practitioners, or better, work done in a community of like-minded professionals. The challenges are formidable but well worth the effort in terms of professional identity and impact on students' growth. Place-based education—through its commitment to shared ownership of the project, process, and outcomes—can counteract the curricular anesthetic, but only if we go past the traditional scripts that dominate modern schooling and make strong, pedagogically driven choices.

CHAPTER 5

Reframing Childhood, Reframing Teaching Practice

Throughout the discussion preceding this chapter, there has been an implicit framing of childhood that needs to be brought forward before wrapping up this analysis. This will lay the foundation for a set of conclusions and recommendations. To start, please recall the earlier discussion of frames from the Preface where the work of Erving Goffman (1986) and Donald Schon (1983) was drawn upon. In simplest terms, frames encompass a set of beliefs or parameters that work to provide a set of conceptual bounds. These bounds in turn help to define the range of choices available to an actor and define what constitutes an acceptable or reasonable choice. At that point the discussion focused on how teachers and parents frame their roles, but it is also useful for our purposes to consider how adults frame the role of the child in society, and in turn how students frame their own identities. As we will see, this mutual framing of childhood explains a lot in regard to how educational decisions get made and programs get implemented. Specific to the context of this book, different frames of childhood serve to enable or constrain the possibilities for place-based education, but by extension the same argument can be applied to other learning opportunities that depend on active student involvement. In any of these efforts, the extent to which we see kids as potentially capable actors—and empower them in fact to be capable—is a prerequisite for success. Programs that rely on but don't successfully activate student agency go nowhere, as we have seen.

As a general statement, it is fair to say that there is a range of opinion at work in American society about just how much agency kids should have, or more simply, how free kids should be in navigating their world independently and in taking on real responsibility. (Since my experience in other cultures is quite limited, readers in other countries will have to filter what follows through their own setting.) Scanning the parenting books at any general-purpose bookstore will make this point quite clear. For every book like *Free-Range Kids* (Skenazy, 2010) touting the benefits of supporting independence and autonomy at a young age, there is another book like *Battle Hymn of the Ti-*

ger Mother (Chua, 2011) advocating a strict, highly structured approach and arguing that we should defer any substantive choice-making until adulthood. With advocates of all stripes available to us, we as a society are conflicted about this issue of childhood agency, a point that is brought home to me whenever I talk with groups of parents. It seems as if there is a continuing quest for balance in kids' lives—the "just right" trade-off of safety and autonomy, communal involvement and pursuit of independent interests, stimulating engagement and time to relax. In practice, it seems that the adult-managed solution tends to win over kids being put in a position to manage their lives. Parents want their kids to be free and confident explorers, but they fear their child becoming a "statistic" after meeting some unknown but greatly feared tragedy. So, exploration and free movement around the community become limited. Likewise, most parents want their kids to develop their own interests and creativity, but at the same time don't want their kids to be left out or left behind. So, kids get overbooked with extracurricular activities so they have a range of experiences leading to a well-rounded if somewhat over-packed education. Even though parents struggle with these issues, the net result for most families in the United States seems to fall on the side of protection and overbooking, with increasing constraints on where kids can go freely and with a much higher portion of non-school time spent in structured programs (Bodilly & Beckett, 2005) than in the past. As we will see, however, these efforts at control and containment are not universal norms of childhood. Other cultures working from different frames of childhood make different choices about kids' safety and about the extent to which their lives are pre-structured by parents and by their schools. To be clear, we're talking about other nations with advanced industrial economies, not some exotic pre-modern culture. There are enough situational similarities in play that it is worth considering what we can learn about childhood as it is lived out in these other relatively similar cultures. It's too easy to say that we should simply adopt other cultures' norms about childhood, but there are aspects worth considering. We live in a global society. We may as well take advantage of it.

Two points that will be put forward in the pages ahead are (1) most kids are safer than we might think, and thus less in need of being enveloped in a security blanket 24/7, and (2) kids are more capable of thinking, deciding, and acting than our currently dominant vision of childhood implies. While they still need adult guidance, we know from the examples provided by many place-based projects that with the right scaffolding in place kids can in fact take on real responsibility even at a comparatively young age. Programming kids' movements as if they were robots needing a script does them a disservice, both for their ability to flourish today and for their ability to grow into increasingly responsible citizens. But in order for place-based education programs to succeed, we need collectively to do a better job of framing childhood as a time when kids can act with increasing levels of agency as they mature toward independence. This is by far the best way for them to build the character, competence, and sense of place needed to act in meaningful ways. They can't stay under wraps and then emerge as full citizens just because they have passed their 18th birthday. Yet in too many cases this is exactly how we act.

Unfortunately for many kids, any wavering and tentative interest that parents may have had in building agency is largely shut out at the school door as institutional norms take over. Instead, with rare exceptions students are expected to conform to a single, quite limiting model with only a few cosmetic variations. The idea that kids can be safe and competent actors in more than narrowly prescribed tasks is largely alien to a typical school environment. Efforts by particularly committed teachers or parents to "move the needle" on giving kids more autonomy draw a strong reaction similar to the way a body reacts to repel antibodies. The infection must be neutralized! It's as if giving kids room to think and to act would lead to chaos. Without a strong school culture of mutual responsibility, it might, but that's an argument for better leadership, not a reason to constrain kids' opportunities.

As is true in all other contexts, the underlying frames of childhood that are operative in schools serve to define the scope of what is reasonable and appropriate, which in turn writes the scripts that many teachers follow. Most American schools—both public and private—are built on an industrial model that focuses on compliance and productivity above all else. While schools will try to deny this or claim that it is an outdated image of schooling ("Look, we have SmartBoards and iPads! Aren't we modern?"), the continuing dominance of the factory metaphor can be seen in a number of features of modern schools. Among the more prominent examples are the school's organizational structures (with assigned, inflexible workstations for teachers and students), the outsized emphasis given to the school accountability movement (with reference to schools' having met or not met performance targets, as if they were fast-food franchises striving to meet sales quotas), and in the rigid adherence to a production schedule (under the guise of a curriculum chart delineating when skills will be mastered, in some cases down to the week or month). These features combine in an act of industrial engineering to create expectations such as "Each fifth grade work unit needs to produce 30 ecology-trained students who can pass a paper test on objectives A–D by the end of the month, investing no more than 30 minutes a day on this process." Teachers who don't deliver mastery among their students as it is defined by this framework are at risk of being replaced. Students who don't perform in this environment face the consequence of spending even more time in the learning environment that has already been demonstrated not to be effective.

The underlying frame at work here is akin to seeing students as raw materials, with teachers as factory line workers charged with production quotas. It is a rare news story about the latest test scores on "student achievement" that actually questions the premises that guide what they are reporting on. Instead, it is taken for granted that the test scores are a real measure of learning, sorting out the good and the bad workers among teachers and students. Actually reporting on this automatic assumption that we are best served by our current testing and accountability frameworks would be akin to the Fish News Network reporting on the presence of water—it's just taken for granted that tests and grades are a natural part of the school ecosystem. Nobody raises questions about it. If we are to support students in rich, place-based instruction, we need to raise the questions of how we frame childhood and learning, and directly related to this, how these frames serve to define the scope and nature of the kids' work and that of their teachers.

Framing Childhood

Since frames of childhood are rarely made explicit in the curriculum documents that guide day-to-day life in schools and in the assessments that purport to measure learning, some of the analysis that follows will be in the form of an "argument by analogy" starting with observations of the dominant frames at work in how we as a society characterize childhood. These observations (again, from a U.S.-based perspective) will then be applied to educational contexts with an eye toward how the frames enable or constrain opportunities for place-based education. It's not hard to see continuities between the dominant cultural views of childhood and their inevitable implementation in school. We will also look at how alternative paradigms of schooling—founded on different frames of childhood—may offer possibilities for place-based learning to thrive. All of this will take us back to our starting point, where we began by reflecting on how differences in teachers' choices and visions enabled some to create rich place-based experiences for kids while others struggled with this task. We'll end with a few summary observations and recommendations.

To start our look at frames of childhood, let's revisit limits on physical navigation of the community. Recall the study wherein successive generations of a British family each had a smaller range of space in which they could roam. My experience and what I see and hear repeatedly from kids and parents tell me that this is much more the norm than the exception. Even within the shrinking areas for exploration that are available to modern kids, the options for play within that space are more and more limited by fears of injury and litigation, and a lack of confidence in kids as problem solvers within a play space. As a result, kids' options are severely limited. Historian Steven Mintz (2004) encapsulates the situation quite effectively as he notes that:

[t]he geography of young people's lives has been reshaped. Much of the "free space" available to youth in the past, from empty lots to nearby woods, has disappeared as a result of development and legal liability concerns. Public playgrounds continue to exist, but as they were childproofed to improve safety, they inadvertently reduced the opportunities for the young to take part in forms of fantasy, sensory, and exploratory play, and construction activities apart from adults. Safety and maintenance concerns led to the removal of sandboxes and swings, metal jungle gyms, and firepoles. Fear of childhood abductions and sexual abuse resulted in the elimination of playgrounds with obstructed views. (p. 348)

We need to move past the fear and prepare kids to live as increasingly responsible members of society. To that end, educator David Sobel (2012) speaks eloquently about managing risk and the danger of our cultural obsession with avoiding any potential harm, since this fear of injury shields kids from having valuable experiences. As he puts it:

Children have been climbing trees for millennia; it's great exercise, and in the vast majority of cases, they don't get hurt. Keep in mind that children get hurt from falls in the bathtub, and we don't prohibit showers. Similarly, children get injured playing competitive sports. We tolerate the risk of injury from field hockey and soccer because we value the physical and social benefits. Why don't we have the same risk/benefit mindset in relation to climbing trees? (para. 22)

The argument, of course, can be extended from climbing trees to many other aspects of childhood experience that we rule out as being too dangerous for kids, or that they just aren't ready to handle at this point in their lives. Implicit in this constriction of young people's space to roam freely is a wide-ranging fear, whether it be of accidental injury, molestation, or physical danger (or perhaps all of the above as a form of generalized anxiety about kids' safety). Whether these fears have a sound basis is questionable, given the fact that violent crime statistics are actually lower than they were in the past (Mintz, 2004), and there is no evidence of great waves of crime being perpetrated against children in cultures which by and large trust kids to handle situations. (Examples of these cultures follow later in this chapter.) Still, news outlets drive their ratings up with sensational stories about dangers posed to kids, which builds a fear among parents. The net result of this is a deeply felt paranoia that limits kids' free exploration. Parents know the risk is one in a million, but they still can't let themselves take that risk. When we weren't saturated with media, our fears weren't stoked by images from far-off places about what horrible things happened to that photogenic kid on the news. The clear implication of each of these news stories is that it could have been your kid, so you'd better be careful. Stay tuned to this station for more details as the case unfolds . . .

In an effort to assess the validity of media hype about dangers to children, sociologist Joel Best (2011) has spent more than two decades maintaining a research program focused on investigating the persistent claims about predatory behavior unleashed on kids in the United States who are trick-or-treating.[1] Even with their ongoing efforts, Best and his research team have been unable to substantiate a single instance of a child being killed or seriously harmed by candy picked up during this popular and playful ritual of childhood. Instead, Best has documented a number of instances in which tragic cases of children dying on or about October 31 were hyped in the media as related to trick-or-treating, but in fact were due to other causes. In the case that may have kicked off the paranoia, it was proved that the 8-year-old boy who died from a cyanide-laced Pixie Stix candy was poisoned by his father, presumably for a large payout of insurance money. The father was subsequently tried and executed for the crime. To buttress his argument that sensationalism is at the heart of this panic, Best maintains an archive of cases in which the media-stoked fears were proved to be unfounded. Still, a 2011 Harris poll found that nearly a quarter of parents retain a fear of what a neighbor might do to their kids on Halloween night.

Even more widespread than the annual fear of Halloween is the ongoing daily fear of a child being molested and/or kidnapped by a stranger. Statistically, "stranger danger" is a quite rare event in comparison with the more real risks kids face. They are nine times as likely to be molested by someone they know such as a family member, teacher, coach, or religious leader than they are by a stranger (American Psychological Association, 2013). Likewise, the danger of a child being kidnapped is most likely attributable to parents in custody disputes (Finkelhor, Hammer, & Sedlak, 2002). While actual risks are minimal, media-inflated risks blare the omnipresent threat as a lurid titillation. Reacting to the fear of kids being unsafe in the neighborhood, we put kids in cars and sign them up for organized programs at distant locations (where, ironically, they are statistically more likely to be abused). Their risk of significant physical injury is likely much higher in the car zipping along the highway than it is building a fort in the woods behind the house. Even if kids are delivered medically intact to the event, the half hour each way spent glued to an iPad as they travel to soccer, baseball, violin, or horse riding is likely much less educative than time spent exploring the neighborhood with friends would be. Frames matter. In this case, a frame that says that kids need to be insulated in a protective barrier changes the nature of how they experience the world.

Expanding a notch or two beyond a fear-driven need to wrap children in layers of protection from society, it's also worth noting that there is a broader lack of trust in kids to be capable actors—to be able to handle situations effectively. I'm not suggesting a Pollyannaish view of childhood that sees a 5-year-old as having the same intellectual and reasoning capacities as an adult and

---

[1] For those not familiar with this phenomenon, dating back at least to my childhood in the 1970s, a non-trivial portion of American parents have been fearful of people poisoning or otherwise tampering with Halloween candy.

who, therefore, should just be left to his own devices and decisions. To be sure, there are individuals and institutions that advocate for a position along those lines. See, for example, free schools like Summerhill (Neill, 1960) or Sudbury Valley (Greenberg, 1995) where even the youngest students can choose their own learning paths and have a vote equal to that of an adult within the school community. Students in these settings can choose to work on whatever intrigues them at the moment (or do basically nothing at all), and can choose to engage or not engage with other teachers and students. While those schools and other settings like that have an admirable trust in young people's capacities, I'm not as sure that is the optimal setting for nurturing development for most kids. Still, their success stories are good, and if it works for those kids and those families, more power to them. Practically speaking, making that kind of child-driven learning environment a necessary condition for a place-based education program would ensure its space on the margins of schooling for the foreseeable future. Schools and our larger culture are just not ready for reform that requires too dramatic a shift in how we see childhood. The recommended changes we are building toward here will be quite enough to present a challenging agenda for parents and schools.

The foundational, non-negotiable idea here is that if we are to better support place-based approaches to education, we need to move past thinking that kids need to be sheltered from the world and that they are incapable of progressive ownership of their learning and their work. Instead, we need to engage kids in the world and give them access to everything they are capable of, and a bit more. In essence, we need to extend the work Rosemary Luckin (2010) has done in adapting teacher work to Vygotksy's zone of proximal development. Recall from Chapter 3 that Luckin coined the term "zone of available assistance" (p. 28) to describe what teachers could do in a supportive environment. It's that extra reach—maybe 10%–20% past current capacity—that is enabled through expert mentoring and support but that wouldn't be accessible without the scaffolding. Similar to this frame for teachers, we need to establish classrooms and communities as zones of more able assistance for kids, providing the scaffolding needed for growth in student ownership of their work and their lives.

The standard response to this might be along the lines of "Of course, that's why we teach kids . . . so they can be independent and do things on their own *later*." I raised the question of student ownership in a recent teacher workshop and drew a strong response from some who feel that they do in fact give their kids autonomy. Examples they gave, though, were still quite limited in terms of real autonomy. For a teacher simply to demonstrate a technique and then give kids time to practice their skills by completing pre-structured problems isn't enough to support students' taking meaningful ownership of their learning. Instead, we need classes and schools where real, valued work is the norm, and teaching supports are in place to scaffold this more complex work. If we are simply teaching a process to be replicated through in-class work, practiced as homework, and then tested, graded, and disposed of, that's not enough. Instead, mentoring toward increased capacity and ownership needs to be in the context of working toward valued outcomes. Here is where the concept of "action competence" described in some detail in the previous chapter comes to the fore. If we are to support meaningful development, kids need a menu of real work along the lines of what was presented in Chapter 4, guided by the pedagogic judgment of their teacher who has a sense of which experiences are most educative. The net result of this shift is that it supports students in building the skills and worldview they need to make a difference in the world. When they do this, they are growing as people, ready to be partici-pants in a democratic society. Simply giving students nominal freedom to work on assignments that feed the wastebasket economy isn't enough.

We can achieve this more meaningful vision of education if we are able to more regularly synthesize many of the key pedagogic ideas underlying place-based education that have been described in the previous chapters. Among the most important of these ideas are (1) Dewey's idea that the teacher has a re-sponsibility to use her experience to guide but not dictate what happens in the classroom (and by extension, in the community), and (2) Hart's ladder of par-ticipation as a road map toward increasing levels of student ownership. When these two ideas get into a productive interplay, good place-based projects can happen since there is mentoring toward increasing students' action compe-tence. As we have seen throughout the book, successful projects are led by teachers who ensure the intellectual, practical, and educational merit of the project, but who also have mastered the art of inviting the students to take ownership at a level that is right for their capacities and experiences. When this happens, the other features of place-based education, including support for character development and pursuit of inquiry, become natural outgrowths. We'll explore more about how this transformed environment reflects a differ-ent frame of childhood in a minute, but first we need to take a look at some predictable objections that might stand in the way.

Can Kids Really Exercise Agency?

It's obvious that this frame of kids as capable actors rubs against the conservative institutional norms of most schools in the United States, and those of many families. Before we dismiss the previous couple of pages as overly optimistic and unworkable, it is important to note that our generally quite limited views of childhood capacity are far from universal, and that there are other advanced industrial cultures that are more trusting of their kids as problem solvers. For example, Gross-Loh (2013) cites examples from her research in a number of other countries ranging from buttoned-down Japan to the more socially open Finland that don't think twice about kids walking to school after being trained at a young age in basic safety procedures. In one telling example of a cultural difference, she relates the story of a Finnish mother who doesn't worry when her 5-year-old daughter runs down the street to see whether a friend is home (or is out elsewhere in the community), but is shocked to read in an online parenting blog the number of American parents who only reluctantly would allow a 14-year-old to go to a skating rink unaccompanied. Lest we write this off as one isolated cultural example, Gross-Loh also documents 6-year-olds in Japan who navigate public transit on their own to get to school, and Swedish kids who simply show up at a field trip location by public transit rather than going to school to get on a bus and travel together with the class. I've observed firsthand Dutch kids roughly 9 or 10 years old as they navigate central Amsterdam by bike on their way to school, without a helmet and with nary a parent nearby.

In none of these cultures is there an epidemic of kidnapping, getting run over in traffic, or getting lost. Arguably, kids who are shuttled and thus don't have to navigate their way through the community are actually at greater risk of getting lost. Here it's worth remembering the trade-off Sobel (2012) discussed, where the benefits of experience are constrained by fear. Referring specifically to the Finnish context, Gross-Loh (2013, p. 206) summarizes the ethos by noting, "Everyone I talked to—parents, educators, and children—emphasized that what characterizes the Finnish way is to give children as much responsibility for their own lives as they can handle." The examples she cites from a range of other countries suggest that it is a frame for childhood that is not idiosyncratic to Finland.

Taken literally, Gross-Loh's last clause about kids having "as much responsibility for their own lives as they can handle" could justify a range of options depending on one's confidence in the child's capacity for autonomy, ranging from an optimistic, laissez-faire Summerhill-like approach that assumes that kids are completely capable, or a very restrictive view that pessimistically assumes virtually no capacity to act independently in an appropriate manner. Looking across a wide range of projects we have supported and others I'm aware of, there is a happy medium needed for place-based learning to thrive. Without question, there is very definitely a role for teachers to play in guiding the scope of the project and ensuring its educational value. To simply turn a project over to the students to drive does a disservice to the students by depriving them of the benefits of the teacher's experience. But not giving the students any real responsibility also does a disservice by failing to nurture growth.

Recall the example of the project connecting local practices in Missouri with the hypoxic "dead zone" in the Gulf of Mexico. While the specific tasks undertaken were do-able by the students, they did not have the background in ecology, economics, and geography needed to see the connections at the be-ginning of their oceanography unit. Drawing on her greater experience and knowledge (and some very skillful pedagogy), their teacher worked with her students to co-create a meaningful project. Similarly, a judicious sense of teacher intervention helped another teacher guide his elementary students in a meaningful investigation of access to healthy food in their community. Given that by and large his students had very little to no experience at school in cre-ating and leading a project, this teacher needed to start where the kids were and give them experiences that were positive in the immediate context and that iteratively built capacity for future leadership as they matured.

A good guideline for practice in place-based education initiatives might be for a teacher to make an honest assessment of where the students are currently located on Hart's ladder of participation, and consider the scaffolding needed for them to move to the next step. Even if our idealistic hopes see students as independent and autonomous project leaders, if they haven't had incremental growth in responsibilities over time it's highly unlikely that they will be able to simply jump up to Hart's highest rungs. Instead, to support growth in capacity over time, we need to give them "as much responsibility for their lives as they can handle" and then just a bit more, scaffolded with mentoring that is with-drawn over time. With the right support, kids very definitely can exercise pro-ductive agency on behalf of projects they believe in.

We have just seen that the relatively constraining frame of childhood typi-cal in the United States is in fact culturally driven and not biologically or de-velopmentally driven. Given this, it's worth considering what factors drive our efforts to contain kids. Our need to control kids' movements and actions may grow out of a well-intended belief that they are just not ready to act. This leads to a fear that if they were left to themselves students would charge forward without the skills and experience they need, only to fail or be injured through their inherent incompetence, hence the ever-present need for protection. Given enough counter-examples from across the globe, though, one could eas-ily argue that much of this relative incompetence has been unintentionally nurtured by not scaffolding increasing levels of responsibility at a younger age. As a simple example, it's unlikely that on her own Susy could find Alexandra's house if she is brought there and back every time in a car. More generally, it would be an interesting study to track how many non-assigned, genuine puz-zles kids get to tease out in a week. In a frame of childhood that—in the name of keeping kids safe—doesn't allow navigation around the neighborhood, con-struction of forts, or exploration of the woods, we shouldn't be surprised if kids don't have good mental maps either of their neighborhood geography or of how things work together. We contain kids at their peril.

If the best preparation for being a 10-year-old is a rich and vital experience as a 9-year-old, we need to be sure that part of that experience is focused on maximizing self-management and self-direction. Schools don't do this very well, and even many parents struggle with it. In many schools, students may need to regulate their body functions to meet official bathroom break times. Even at home, when we schedule every minute of a child's day and transport him everywhere wrapped in a motor vehicle, we're treating the kids as cargo, not as actors who are building a sense of agency in the world. If we give them no choices, they will give us no plans. Change in this realm will be difficult in that it requires a philosophical shift in how we see childhood and an operational change in how we gradually share authority with kids, but it is do-able. For this change to happen, though, we need to lose some of our fear and our need for containment, and work toward a greater understanding of how to nurture ongoing development. Examples from other cultures suggest that there are options in how we structure youth experiences. This isn't to suggest that we simply adopt another country's norms, as if that were even possible. We will likely still have differences, but we can use others' experiences to consider new paths. What we need is for these paths to be consciously chosen and not simply be the default setting of "how children are" or "what kids need today" emerging out of a lack of awareness of different frames.

Can Kids Be Trusted?

I fear, however, that there is more at work here than just an issue of awareness in how schools and many families constrain kids. Instead, there is a pernicious view lurking in American culture that when taken only a step or two further sees children as wild beasts who must be trained and controlled. All too often, we don't give them responsibility because we don't trust them—especially in school. While we are gradually moving away from the puritanical view of children having inborn evil that needs to be whipped out of them, we are still a long way from eradicating the underlying mindset that kids need to be civilized through coercion. People who doubt this should wander into a Christian book store some day and peruse the parenting titles. While some actually retain the puritanical flogging streak, even more betray a mindset of instant, complete, and unquestioning obedience to adult authority. For example, Michael and Debi Pearl relate the example of an infant being held against his will at an adult church meeting. As you can imagine, the expected squirming and grabbing for diversions took place, causing the Pearls (2006) to comment, "It was enough to make you believe the Devil started out as an infant . . . . It causes one to understand where the concept of a 'sinful nature' originated" (p. 14). They continue, describing that child's life as "one of unlimited, unrestrained self-indulgence." The clear implication is that the infant sinned in not choosing to be properly respectful of adult authority by displaying appropriate meeting etiquette.

Lest we think this is unique to fundamentalist culture, historian Philip Greven (1990) traces this puritanical mindset toward childhood throughout American history. As he notes, there is an ethos of breaking wills that is seen as "essential to the creation of morality, spirituality, and character, and vital, ultimately, to the salvation of souls" (p. 61). Clearly kids need guidance in learning to sublimate their own desires at times in order to work collaboratively within the larger culture, but this is a mentoring process with a long-term goal of building increasing capacity for social intelligence, not a mandate for breaking a child's will that is by nature assumed to be recalcitrant. Returning to Gross-Loh's (2013) international study, one of the recurring themes is how parents and teens in many other cultures are surprised by the assumption in the United States that there is an inherent opposition between kids and parents. Relationships between generations don't need to be antagonistic.

Beyond the family, there is still a mindset of control and coercion at work, coupled with an assumed lack of competence among the young that prevents them from acting within society in a meaningful way. There is an underlying cultural ethos that if you are a "good kid" and behave, you will be protected from any real responsibility, but if you mess up, watch out. You will be punished severely. Relative to this point, it's a sad irony that one of the few times in the United States that we allow people under 18 to take legal responsibility is when they are charged with a crime. Then it's OK to charge them as an adult. In fact, it has only been a few years since the U.S. Supreme Court ruled that people couldn't be executed for a crime committed at a point in their lives when they were considered too young to make an informed choice about buying a $1 lottery ticket. As another indication of how we as a country see childhood as a time for complete adult control, it's important to note that the United States is one of only two United Nations member countries that doggedly refuses to sign on to the U.N. Declaration of the Rights of the Child. We and Somalia stand alone on this. Objections to ratifying the charter center on a fear that kids having their own rights would interfere with parental rights to control and discipline their kids as they see fit. Countering this, there is a national movement to ratify a Parental Rights Amendment to the United States Constitution. Taking the control issue to the point of absurdity, in Texas part of the official Republican Party platform seeks to outlaw teaching higher-order thinking in school, since this would "have the purpose of challenging the student's fixed beliefs and undermining parental authority" (Republican Party of Texas, 2012, p. 10). Where would we be if education were to provide an opportunity to reflect on and further develop what one thought?

Clearly we have odd mismatches at work in how we see childhood and how we think about education, with concerns about controlling kids—whether it is for protection or for punishment—taking precedence over concerns about empowering and building social competence. While we have to be careful not to extrapolate too far from these extreme examples, we need to take note of the way they shine light on a broader, largely negative and constraining view of childhood that is far from rare in our culture, and not very far from the surface. While we're hardly the first generation to distrust the young and see them as somehow less worthy successors to our generation's example (Mintz, 2004), we need to do better. Fortunately, not everyone sees kids in such a suspicious light, but practically speaking, the dominance of this negative and constraining frame of childhood works against creating a climate that respects kids as autonomous and capable actors. As a result, it becomes harder to establish the essential groundwork needed for place-based education to take root. To the extent that we don't respect and trust children as autonomous and intelligent beings working toward independent citizenship, it is very hard to realize the ambitious vision of education encompassed in place-based approaches. Instead, we maintain a school environment focused on containing the kids and feeding them bite-sized nuggets of knowledge that we think they are capable of digesting.

As an illustration of control in action, I've worked with teachers in schools where all of the students walk silently in the halls no more than an elbow's length from the wall. While this example of restrictive coercion is particularly extreme, rules of that ilk are hardly unheard of. The Assertive Discipline classroom management program (Canter, 2009)—now in its fourth edition—remains popular in schools. While billed as "positive behavior management," in practice it is very one-directional in establishing, communicating, and enforcing rules on the students. While we have (mostly) moved from paddles and switches to lectures about behavior and restricted privileges in school, it's still a model of aggressive imposition rather than collaborative maintenance of a productive learning environment. Even in nominally more open environments, if there isn't a basic trust in the kids then the underlying ethos of control will surface. A teacher at a school near Boston told me recently that they generally let the kids go to the bathroom by themselves, except during testing weeks. She wasn't sure whether this policy was out of concern that a student on the loose might be disruptive during the high holy days of testing, or whether it was out of concern for a 9-year-old's cheating ring. In either case, the test-week policy conveys a lack of trust and respect for the kids as social actors.[2] If we can't trust kids with a basic task such as walking safely and civilly down the hall, it's inconceivable that they can be expected to act with autonomy and social awareness in other realms. Can we trust them to work out in the community?

Again, we need to be careful not to let this drip into a Pollyannaish view of kids as being inherently virtuous and self-managing. The teacher does need

---

[2] Note the implied lack of respect for the teachers in that school, being expected to enforce a rule for which they weren't made aware of the rationale.

to provide leadership and is ultimately responsible for classroom management, but it can be done in a way that builds autonomy and self-direction. This is something that schools with a more positive, child-centered frame do well. When I worked at the Atrium School, a progressive school just outside of Boston, the entire school ran on one "respect" rule. The extended commentary amounted to "respect yourselves, respect others, respect the environment." Seven words, three of which were repeated. It's hard to think of responsibility and behavior issues that come up in school that wouldn't be covered by one of those clauses or by the overarching commitment to respect as a behavioral norm. Similarly, the Odyssey School—a "magnet" environmental school in Denver—also runs on three basic behavioral norms. The expectation there is that a student should make choices that are kind, safe, and appropriate. The key differences in both of these cases when compared with a more traditional authoritarian management style are that the norms are jointly held and maintained by the teacher and the students, and that transgressions lead to informal coaching, not harsh will-breaking consequences. A more optimistic frame that kids can be trusted and held to being their best selves leads to different experiences.

As noted at the outset of this chapter, there is a diversity of opinion within the parenting world about how much autonomy kids should have. Even there, though, we have seen a marked tendency toward constraint based on fear and lack of confidence in kids' ability—even in the teen years—to make sound and capable decisions. With the exception of occasional schools founded on more progressive principles, even this modest diversity that parents hold in frames of childhood seems lost at the schoolhouse door. While values such as autonomy and judgment are paid lip service, it is clear to anyone who spends much time in schools that kids have even less room to develop and act on any sense of agency than do their highly scripted teachers. Everyone—teacher and student alike—is expected to fall into the cheerful robot mode.

And the Relevance Is . . . ?

This extended focus on youth agency can be summarized in one sentence: If kids are to move to the higher rungs on Hart's ladder of participation, they need to be seen and supported as increasingly capable actors at home and at school. Recall Dewey's assertion in *My Pedagogic Creed* (1897/1964) when he argued that:

> [t]he teacher is not in the school to impose certain ideas or to form certain habits in the child, but is there as a member of the community to select the influences which

shall affect the child and to assist him in properly responding to these influences. (p. 432)

With very few apologies to the Texas Republican Party, this isn't a bad job description for parents and other caregivers as well. The same 14-year-old who isn't trusted to go to a skating rink by herself is unlikely to have been nurtured over the years to develop the independent thought needed to be part of a team working in the community toward valued ends. Echoing the Finnish parent cited earlier in this chapter, we really do need to give kids as much control of their lives as possible.

Realizing the educational benefits of high-quality place-based projects requires strong youth agency, which assumes a more active stance in the world. Assumptions of childhood characterized by fragility, incompetence, and a basic heathen nature work against framing childhood for agency. Students cannot engage in meaningful service-learning, nor can they build action competence, if they are not part of the effort to identify and choose the activities undertaken, and if they have no hand in structuring the actual involvement. We can and need to do better in giving kids these experiences. Of course there are developmental issues at work here, but even young students can consider options and raise ideas for how they can have an impact on their community ("If we want more butterflies, we should have more flowers . . ."). Pre-teens have more capacity than do younger students, and thus are able to start making more complex plans. Even here there are limits, but with good leadership the developmental issues can be worked with.

As I mentioned earlier, for the past couple of years I have co-led a place-based church youth group for 10- to 12-year-olds that spends much of its time engaged in learning about community issues such as access to food and animal care, and engaging in related community projects. For a recent animal theme— which they chose—they wanted to literally adopt an animal. This wasn't to be one of those quasi-adoptions where you raise money for a zoo animal and get a picture to take home. They wanted actual custody of Fido or Fluffy. Here we as the youth group leaders had to exercise a bit of adult judgment and help the kids to see the full implications of their idea. Who would care for the animal other than the one hour each week we were together? The kids countered with a rotation moving the adopted pet daily from house to house. As they articulated this, other group members raised the point that it wouldn't be fair to the pet to be shuttled from house to house, and that the pet would likely live for many years after our time together as a youth group ended. After some discussion the kids realized that their plan would be unfair to the pet, and they moved on to other plans to support shelter animals and encourage lasting adoptions among members of the congregation.

The key point here is that the entire experience relied on an underlying frame that has confidence in the kids as being capable of making guided choices and able to chart a path for their efforts, both at the macro level (their four-month focus on animals as the thematic organizer for their work), and at the micro level (in how specific activities were chosen, implemented, and evaluated). Scripted paths chosen for kids will not help them to develop their capacity to think through issues and make wise choices. Assuming that our making choices for them will provide a model they can use when they are old enough to choose is optimistic to say the least. In practice, it undermines the agency they need for democratic citizenship.

Looking at the other building blocks of strong place-based programs, it should be clear how differences in ways childhood is framed affect the roles students take, and how far they can move up on Hart's ladder of participation as they mature. On one hand, an annual food drive where everyone is encouraged to bring in canned goods and the kids box things up for the local food pantry is a nice photo op for the school newsletter, but it serves to tokenize the kids if it is not part of a larger effort to understand and respond to food insecurity in the community. On the other hand, if the kids were to look at multiple options for making a difference in the community, select the food pantry as their focus, and learn enough to credibly educate the school community about local food issues, they would be engaged in a much more meaningful project. Academically, a project such as this would provide a range of language and math skills development opportunities, as well as a chance to gain meaningful access to the "global knowledge inheritance" that we all draw from. Throughout, the kids build moral, civic, performance, and intellectual character as they design, implement, and monitor the progress of their project. But it all relies on a frame of childhood that sees kids as capable of acting within the community in a safe and productive manner.

Seeing Kids as Capable Thinkers and Doers: The Most Challenging Script of All?

Earlier we looked at the scripts that many teachers follow as they go about their work, held to tightly woven pacing charts and similar planning documents, and bound by conventions of what it means to be a teacher. In response, students all too often act on passive scripts of their own relating to what they need to do in carrying out their role with a minimum of friction. Go through the motions, keep your head down, and get through the day seems to be a survival mantra for many students. This move toward inactivity grows over time as students progress through the grades, with the bright-eyed kindergartener turning into the moody teen and the passive college student whose primary concern is whether something in class will be on the test. It is said that every parent's wish for schools is encapsulated in a simple request:

"We send our children off to kindergarten as bright-eyed, inquisitive learners. Please return them that way when you are done with them." This pattern of controlling and constraining isn't universal, of course, but it is common enough to warrant concern and necessitate our best thinking on creating a more promising alternative. For more active learning environments to take root and flourish, we need a richer paradigm of childhood to frame our thinking. Given the extent to which frames serve to validate some options over others, this new paradigm in turn will help to create new roles both for teachers and for students. It is to that task we now turn as we wrap up the book.

Given the centrality of the scripts many teachers work from, and the ways in which they often serve to constrain experience, we need new scripts if we are going to achieve new visions of teaching and learning. We might even need to discard the script metaphor completely and do a better job of empowering teachers to improvise more, informed by real professional expertise. Acting on these issues may well fill a successor volume to this offering, but for now we'll close with a sketch of what is needed. This analysis draws primarily on work done by Nobel Prize–winning psychologist Daniel Kahnemann (2011) and his colleague the late Amos Tversky. Kahnemann argues that we generally make quick, intuitive decisions with our System 1 brains, which seem set up to deflect us from too much deep analytical thinking with our System 2 brains. Thus, a teacher workshop that provides all kinds of advanced tools and all the right reasons for using them won't be effective if our System 1 brain is deeply embedded in a frame of teaching that doesn't embrace such an approach. In a sense, System 1 bats away the distractions, keeping them from ever reaching deep cogitation by System 2. If we are required to, we tolerate the introjection of the new rule into our life and give outward compliance (Deci & Flaste, 1995), but only until we can get back to what we "know" is the right way to teach. Our System 1 minds, our gut instincts, or our scripts if you will, make most of our decisions for us. Kahnemann argues that this reliance on System 1 takes place for good reason, as we usually can't stop and analyze deeply all of the many ramifications of a decision. As I noted earlier, we don't have time to do a literature review on the best current understanding on how to redirect Johnny's off-task behavior. So, our System 1 brain makes the decision quickly and effortlessly, reflecting whatever educational values it is populated by.

This premise of quick, almost intuitive thinking as defining our practice has huge implications for how well and how much we can move "in-service" teachers toward a different frame of teaching. The durable notion throughout this book has been that how we frame our work determines in large part how we function. In-service workshops that focus on activity training, curriculum coverage, or preparation for testing reinforce the traditional teaching script, which as we have seen is founded on values that run counter to student autonomy and engagement. Given that teachers are going to make relatively automatic System 1 decisions in their practice, we need to develop strategies that shift their professional frames. The default answer for a teacher needs to lean toward a professional identity of helping kids to be engaged in the community and scaffolding students' ownership, not simply on rote compliance with curriculum standards and test scores. This will require digging in deeply to change the more consciously chosen System 2 beliefs that inform the more automatic and intuitive System 1 responses. Specific to the focus of this book, if place-based values don't penetrate deeply into the teacher's identity, efforts to impose place-based education as a new reform will just be an introjection that will be co-opted to serve the teacher's existing mindset or discarded as soon as possible.

Left to its own devices, the modern framing of school reduces teachers to the functional equivalent of a factory line worker churning out educational products that meet the quality specifications covered in the district pacing charts and in students' test results. Instead, a teacher needs to become a craftsperson of sorts (Sennett, 2008), making iterative improvements that draw on a wealth of experience with the materials and tools at hand. Just as an experienced woodcrafter draws on a wealth of prior experience, teachers also benefit from their time spent immersed in problems of practice (Claxton, 1997). Thinking through options alone and in consultation with peers is an essential function of a craftsperson. To do their jobs well, teachers need to roll up their sleeves and carve out great learning spaces in collaboration with the kids. In an Aristotelian sense, they need to exercise phronesis, or practical wisdom, as much or more than they do techne, or technical reasoning. Building agency and ownership with kids is as much or more a matter of applied wisdom as it is a measurable process.

Operationally speaking, it will help if administrators and the larger systems of which they are a part can better support this revised frame that sees teaching as a process of exercising wisdom on behalf of student agency. If active support for teachers' own agency is hard at the moment, we need to at least stop suppressing it so that teachers can better exercise decision making on behalf of their students. I'm skeptical that we will see a widespread shift in teacher behavior right away, both because of the extent to which traditional teaching scripts are embedded in norms of practice and because these scripts themselves are embedded in even more deeply held norms of childhood. Still, we need to start somewhere. Providing the space for movement in the right direction is an essential first step. Teachers need to be supported in reflecting on their practice to develop within their System 2 minds a commitment to youths' capacities for character and competence development, and to nurturing kids' sense of place. Teachers also need support in applying this deliberately chosen worldview as they make the many instantaneous decisions that are part of the job. Each project a teacher undertakes can be an opportunity for subtle but significant shifts in practice toward norms such as more student ownership of the learning and toward knowledge being seen as more than facts and procedures to be replicated on demand. As these small changes happen over time, there will be a shifting of the educational ground toward norms and values that allow place-based and similar programs to take root in schools and thrive.

In terms of professional development specifically for place-based education, how do we design experiences that will challenge teachers to start changing the deep thinking that underlies their practice? This won't be easy, but fortunately there are established professional development models that will be useful for this purpose. To that end, we'll close with a few key markers of what is likely needed for lasting change: In place of formulaic in-service workshops, teachers need sustained experiences with coaching and co-teaching under the guidance of mentor teachers (Joyce & Showers, 2002). Done well, place-based education calls on us to invest ourselves in the work, sharing our passions and interests with the kids. This requires more than just technical execution of lesson plans in a timely manner to achieve good test scores. Throughout, greater attention needs to be paid to how the personal and professional relate. All of this suggests that we need professional development experiences that help teachers consider the personal and social dimensions of their practice, not just the technical acts (Bell & Gilbert, 1996). Most foundationally, we need to help teachers see how their System 2 theoretical commitments play out through System 1 in practice (Adey, 2004). To the extent that teacher identities are held deeply as part of one's personal and professional identity, change in teaching goals and values will take time. But it is worthy work to help students develop the capacity and commitment they need to function in a modern democratic society. As such, it is an effort deserving of our support.

References

Abbott, E. A. (1994). *Flatland*. New York, NY: HarperCollins.

Adey, P. (2004). *The professional development of teachers: Practice and theory*. Dordrecht, The Netherlands: Kluwer Academic.

American Psychological Association. (2013). Child sexual abuse: What parents should know. Available at http://www.apa.org/pi/families/resources/child-sexual-abuse.aspx. Retrieved September 9, 2013.

Audet, R., & Ludwig, G. (2000). *GIS in schools*. Redlands, CA: ESRI Press.

Baehr, J. (2013). Educating for intellectual virtues: From theory to practice. *Journal of Philosophy of Education, 47*(2), 248–262.

Bateson, G. (2000). *Steps to an ecology of mind*. Chicago, IL: University of Chicago Press.

Bell, B., & Gilbert, J. (1996). *Teacher development: A model from science education*. London, UK: Falmer Press.

Bell, P., & Linn, M. (2002). Beliefs about science: How does science instruction contribute? In B. K. Hofer & P. R. Pintrich (Eds.), *Personal epistemology: The psychology of beliefs about knowledge and knowing* (pp. 321–346). Mahwah, NJ: Lawrence Erlbaum Associates.

Best, J. (2011). Halloween sadism: The evidence. Available at http://udspace.udel.edu/handle/19716/726. Retrieved September 9, 2013.

Bodilly, S., & Beckett, M. K. (2005). *Making out-of-school-time matter: Evidence for an action agenda*. Santa Monica, CA: Rand Corporation.

Borman, G. D., & Kimball, S. M. (2004). *Teacher quality and educational equality: Do teachers with higher standards-based evaluation ratings close student achievement gaps?* Consortium for Policy Research in Education CPRE Working Paper Series TC-04003. Available at cpre.wceruw.org/papers/teacher_equity_aera04.pdf. Retrieved November 15, 2012.

Canter, L. (2009). *Assertive discipline: Positive behavior management for today's classroom* (4th ed.). Bloomington, IN: Solution Tree.

Chawla, L. (2009). Growing up green: Becoming an agent of care for the natural world. *Journal of Developmental Processes, 4*(1), 6–23.

Chua, A. (2011). *Battle hymn of the tiger mother*. New York, NY: Penguin.

Claxton, G. (1997). *Hare brain, tortoise mind*. New York, NY: HarperCollins.

Comstock, A. B. (1986). *Handbook of nature study*. Ithaca, NY: Cornell University Press.

Coulter, B. (2000a). Investigating an urban watershed: How healthy is Deer Creek? In R. Audet & G. Ludwig (Eds.), *GIS in schools* (pp. 55–62). Redlands, CA: ESRI Press.

Coulter, B. (2000b). What's it like where you live? Meeting the standards through technology enhanced inquiry. *Science and Children, 37*(4), 46–50.

Coulter, B. (2012). Launching investigations with bite-sized gaming. In S. Dikkers, J. Martin, & B. Coulter (Eds.), *Mobile media learning: Amazing uses of mobile devices for learning* (pp. 61–76). Pittsburgh, PA: ETC Press.

Deci, E. L., & Flaste, R. (1995). *Why we do what we do.* New York, NY: Penguin Press.

Deci, E. L., & Ryan, R. M. (Eds.). (2002). *Handbook of self-determination theory.* Rochester, NY: University of Rochester Press.

Dewey, J. (1897/1964). My pedagogic creed. In R. D. Archambault (Ed.), *John Dewey on education: Selected writings* (pp. 442–439). Chicago, IL: University of Chicago Press.

Dewey, J. (1902/1990). *The school and society.* Chicago, IL: University of Chicago Press.

Dewey, J. (1929/1988). *The quest for certainty* (The later works of John Dewey 1925–1953, vol. 4). Carbondale, IL: Southern Illinois University Press.

Dewey, J. (1934/2005). *Art as experience.* New York, NY: Perigree Books.

Dewey, J. (1938a/1963). *Experience and education.* New York, NY: Collier Books.

Dewey, J. (1938b). *Logic: The theory of inquiry.* New York, NY: Henry Holt.

Dikkers, S., Martin, J., & Coulter, B. (Eds). (2012). *Mobile media learning: Amazing uses of mobile devices for learning.* Pittsburgh, PA: ETC Press.

Emirbayer, M., & Mische, A. (1998). What is agency? *American Journal of Sociology, 103*(4), 962–1023.

Freire, P. (1993). *Pedagogy of the oppressed.* New York, NY: Continuum.

Feldman, A., Konold, C., & Coulter, B. (2000). *Network science a decade later: The Internet and classroom learning.* Mahwah, NJ: Lawrence Erlbaum Associates.

Ferkany, M., & Whyte, K. P. (2011). Environmental education, wicked problems and virtue. *Philosophy of Education.* Available at http://ssrn.com/abstract=1761029. Retrieved June 22, 2013.

Ferkany, M., & Whyte, K. P. (2012). The importance of participatory virtues in the future of environmental education. *Journal of Agricultural and Environmental Ethics, 25*(3), 419–434.

Feucht, F. C., & Bendixen, L. D. (2010). A welcome and guide for the reader. In L. C. Bendixen & F. C. Feucht (Eds.), *Personal epistemology in the classroom: Theory, research, and implications for practice* (pp. 3–28). Cambridge, UK: Cambridge University Press.

Finkelhor, D., Hammer, H., & Sedlak, A. J. (2002, October). Nonfamily abducted children: National estimates and characteristics. *National Incidence Studies of Missing, Abducted, Runaway, and Thrownaway Children.* Washington, DC: U.S. Department of Justice. Available at http://www.missingkids.com/en_US/documents/nismart2_nonfamily.pdf. Retrieved September 9, 2013.

Goffman, E. (1986). *Frame analysis.* Boston, MA: Northeastern University Press.

Greenberg, D. (1995). *Free at last: The Sudbury Valley School.* Framingham, MA: Sudbury Valley School Press.

Gresalfi, M., Barnes, J., & Cross, D. (2012). When does an opportunity become an opportunity? Unpacking classroom practice through the lens of ecological psychology. *Educational Studies in Mathematics, 80*(1–2), 249–267.

Greven, P. (1991). *Spare the child: The religious roots of punishment and the psychological impact of physical abuse.* New York, NY: Alfred A. Knopf.

Gross-Loh, C. (2013). *Parenting without borders: Surprising lessons parents around the world can teach us.* New York, NY: Penguin.

Hart, R. (1997). *Children's participation.* London, UK: Earthscan.

Hillman, M., Adams, J., & Whitelegg, J. (1990). *One false move . . . a study of children's independent mobility*. London, UK: Policy Studies Institute. Available at http://john-adams.co.uk/wp-content/uploads/2007/11/one%20false%20move.pdf. Retrieved September 4, 2013.

Hirsch, E. D. (1988). *Cultural literacy: What every American needs to know*. New York, NY: Vintage.

Huizinga, J. (1971). *Homo ludens: A study of the play-element in culture*. Boston, MA: Beacon Press.

Hutchison, D. (2004). *A natural history of place in education*. New York, NY: Teachers College Press.

Jensen, B. B. (2004). Environmental and health education viewed from an action-oriented perspective: A case from Denmark. *Journal of Curriculum Studies, 36*(4), 405–425.

Jensen, B. B., & Schnack, K. (1997). The action competence approach in environmental education. *Environmental Education Research, 3*(2), 163–178.

Johnson, B., Duffin, M., & Murphy, M. (2012). Quantifying a relationship between place-based learning and environmental quality. *Environmental Education Research, 18*(5), 609–624.

Johnston, J. S. (2008). *Deweyan inquiry*. Albany, NY: SUNY Press.

Joyce, B., & Showers, B. (2002). *Student achievement through staff development* (3rd ed.). Alexandria, VA: Association for Supervision and Curriculum Development.

Kahnemann, D. (2011). *Thinking fast and slow*. New York, NY: Farrar, Straus & Giroux.

Kliebard, H. M. (2004). *The struggle for the American curriculum* (3rd ed). New York, NY: Routledge.

Klopfer, E. (2008). *Augmented learning: Research and design of mobile games*. Cambridge, MA: MIT Press.

Krulwich, R. (2012). Do you know where your children are? Is that always a good thing? Available at http://www.npr.org/blogs/krulwich/2012/10/01/162079442/. Retrieved October 15, 2012.

Kuhn, D., & Weinstock, M. (2002). What is epistemological thinking and why does it matter? In B. K. Hofer & P. R. Pintrich (Eds.), *Personal epistemology: The psychology of beliefs about knowledge and knowing* (pp. 121–144). Mahwah, NJ: Lawrence Erlbaum Associates.

Lachs, J. (2012). *Stoic pragmatism*. Bloomington, IN: Indiana University Press.

Laurillard, D. (2012). *Teaching as a design science*. New York, NY: Routledge.

Lave, J. (1988). *Cognition in practice: Mind, mathematics and culture in everyday life*. Cambridge, UK: Cambridge University Press.

Lawler. R. W., & Rushby, N. (2013). An interview with Robert Lawler. *British Journal of Educational Technology, 44*(1), 20–30.

Lemann, N. (1998, November 5). Ready, READ! *Atlantic Monthly, 282*. Available at http://www.theatlantic.com/past/docs/issues/98nov/read.htm. Retrieved September 4, 2013.

Lieberman, G. A., & Hoody, L. L. (1998). *Closing the achievement gap*. San Diego, CA: State Education and Environment Roundtable.

Linn, M. C., & Hsi, S. (2000). *Computers, teachers, peers: Science learning partners*. Mahwah, NJ: Lawrence Erlbaum Associates.

Lipton, P. (1991). *Inference to the best explanation*. London, UK: Routledge.

Lockhart, P. (2009). *A mathematician's lament: How school cheats us out of our most fascinating and imaginative art form*. New York, NY: Bellevue Literary Press.

Louv, R. (2005). *Last child in the woods: Saving our children from nature-deficit disorder*. Chapel Hill, NC: Algonquin Books.

Lowe, R. (2007). *The death of progressive education: How teachers lost control of the classroom*. London, UK: Routledge.

Luckin, R. (2010). *Redesigning learning contexts*. New York, NY: Routledge.

Malcolm, S. (1990). Local action for a better environment. Quoted in J. Palmer & P. Neal (1994), *The handbook of environmental education*. New York, NY: Routledge.

Martin, L. M. W. (2000). The compatibility of Vygotsky's theoretical framework with the developmental-interaction approach. In N. Nager & E. K. Shapiro (Eds.), *Revisiting a progressive pedagogy: The developmental-interaction approach*. Albany, NY: SUNY Press.

May, M. E. (2010). *In pursuit of elegance*. New York, NY: Broadway Books.

Mintz, S. (2004). *Huck's raft: A history of American childhood*. Cambridge, MA: Belknap Press.

Mills, C. W. (1959/2000). *The sociological imagination*. Oxford, UK: Oxford University Press.

Mitchell, L. S. (1963/2001). *Young geographers*. New York, NY: Bank Street College of Education.

Nager, N., & Shapiro, E. K. (Eds.). (2000). *Revisiting a progressive pedagogy: The developmental-interaction approach*. Albany, NY: SUNY Press.

National Youth Leadership Council. (2008). *K–12 service-learning standards for quality practice*. St. Paul, MN: Author.

Neill, A. S. (1960). *Summerhill: A radical approach to child rearing*. New York, NY: Hart.

Palmer, J., & Neal, P. (1994). *The handbook of environmental education*. New York, NY: Routledge.

Papert, S. (1994). *The children's machine*. New York, NY: Basic Books.

Patri, A. (1997). *A schoolmaster of the great city*. New York, NY: New Press.

Pearl, M., & Pearl, D. (2006). *To train up a child*. Pleasantville, TN: NGJ Ministries.

Pignatelli, F. (2000). Furthering a progressive agenda: Advisement and the development of educators. In N. Nager & E. K. Shapiro (Eds.), *Revisiting a progressive pedagogy: The developmental-interaction approach* (pp. 221–238). Albany, NY: SUNY Press.

Place-Based Education Evaluation Collaborative. (2010). *The benefits of place-based education: A report from the Place-based Education Evaluation Collaborative* (2nd ed.). Available at http://tinyurl.com/PEECBrochure. Retrieved September 4, 2013.

Polman, J. (2004). *Designing project-based science: Connecting learners through guided inquiry*. New York, NY: Teachers College Press.

Pritchard, D. (2013). Epistemic virtue and the epistemology of education. *Journal of Philosophy of Education, 47*(2), 236–247.

Reeve, J. (2002). Self-determination theory applied to educational settings. In E. L. Deci & R. M. Ryan (Eds.), *Handbook of self-determination research* (pp. 183–204). Rochester, NY: University of Rochester Press.

Republican Party of Texas. (2012). *Report of platform committee*. Available at http://s3.amazonaws.com/texasgop_pre/assets/original/2012Platform_Final.pdf. Retrieved August 18, 2013.

Ripley, A. (2013). *The smartest kids in the world and how they got that way*. New York, NY: Simon & Schuster.

Rheingold, A., & Seaman, J. (2013, April). *The use-value of real-world projects: Children and community-based experts connecting through school work*. Paper presented at the annual meeting of the American Educational Research Association (AERA), San Francisco, CA.

Rosenholtz, S. (1991). *Teachers' workplace: The social organization of schools*. New York, NY: Teachers College Press.

Sahlberg, P. (2011). *Finnish lessons: What can the world learn from educational change in Finland?* New York, NY: Teachers College Press.

Schine, C. (2013). *Fin and lady*. New York, NY: Farrar, Straus & Giroux.

Schommer-Aikens, M. (2002). An evolving theoretical framework for an epistemological belief system. In B. K. Hofer & P. R. Pintrich (Eds.), *Personal epistemology: The psychology of beliefs about knowledge and knowing* (pp. 103–118). Mahwah, NJ: Lawrence Erlbaum Associates.

Schon, D. (1983). *The reflective practitioner.* New York, NY: Basic Books.

Schusler, T. M., Krasny, M. E., Peters, S. J., & Decker, D. J. (2009). Developing citizens and communities through youth environmental action. *Environmental Education Research, 15*(1), 208–223.

Sennett, R. (2008). *The craftsman.* New Haven, CT: Yale University Press.

Shaffer, D. W., & Gee, J. P. (2006). *How computer games help children learn.* New York, NY: Palgrave Macmillan.

Shapiro, E., & Biber, B. (1972). The education of young children: A developmental-interaction approach. *Teachers College Record, 74*(1), 55–79.

Shields, D. L. (2011). Character as the aim of education. *Kappan, 92*(8), 48–53.

Sidorkin, A. M. (2010). *Labor of learning: Market and the next generation of educational reform.* Rotterdam, The Netherlands: Sense.

Skenazy, L. (2010). *Free-range kids: How to raise safe, self-reliant children (without going nuts with worry).* San Francisco, CA: Jossey-Bass.

Smith, G. A. (2013). Place-based education. In R. B. Stevenson, M. Brody, J. Dillon, & A. E. J. Wals (Eds.), *International handbook of research on environmental education* (pp. 213–220). New York, NY: Routledge.

Sobel, D. (1996). *Beyond ecophobia: Reclaiming the heart in nature education* (Nature Literacy Monograph Series No. 1). Great Barrington, MA: Orion Society.

Sobel, D. (2004). *Place-based education: Connecting classrooms and communities.* Great Barrington, MA: Orion Society.

Sobel, D. (2011). *Wild play: Parenting adventures in the great outdoors.* San Francisco, CA: Sierra Club.

Sobel, D. (2012, July–August). Look, don't touch: The problem with environmental education. *Orion.* Available at http://www.orionmagazine.org/index.php/articles/article/6929. Retrieved September 7, 2013.

Stein, M. K., Smith, M. S., Henningsen, M., & Silver, E. A. (2009). *Implementing standards-based mathematics instruction* (2nd ed.). New York, NY: Teachers College Press.

Tanner, L. N. (1997). *Dewey's Laboratory School: Lessons for today.* New York, NY: Teachers College Press.

Timmermans, S., & Tavory, I. (2012). Theory construction in qualitative research: From grounded theory to abductive analysis. *Sociological Theory, 30*(3), 167–186.

Tyack, D., & Cuban, L. (1997). *Tinkering toward Utopia.* Cambridge, MA: Harvard University Press.

Vascellaro, S. (2011). *Out of the classroom and into the world.* New York, NY: New Press.

Yazzie-Mintz, E. (2010). *Charting the path from engagement to achievement: A report on the 2009 high school survey of student engagement,* Available at http://ceep.indiana.edu/hssse/images/HSSSE_2010_Report.pdf. Retrieved March 7, 2011.

GENERAL EDITORS: CONSTANCE RUSSELL & JUSTIN DILLON

The [Re]thinking Environmental Education book series is a response to the international recognition that environmental issues have taken center stage in political and social discourse. Resolution and/or re-evaluation of the many contemporary environmental issues will require a thoughtful, informed, and well-educated citizenry. Quality environmental education does not come easily; it must be grounded in mindful practice and research excellence. This series reflects the highest quality of contemporary scholarship and, as such, is positioned at the leading edge not only of the field of environmental education, but of education generally. There are many approaches to environmental education research and delivery, each grounded in particular contexts and epistemological, ontological and axiological positions, and this series reflects that diversity.

For additional information about this series or for the submission of manuscripts, please contact:

Constance Russell & Justin Dillon
c/o Peter Lang Publishing, Inc.
29 Broadway, 18th floor
New York, New York 10006

To order other books in this series, please contact our Customer Service Department:

(800) 770-LANG (within the U.S.)
(212) 647-7706 (outside the U.S.)
(212) 647-7707 FAX

Or browse by series:

WWW.PETERLANG.COM